Joyce Stranger was born in London but has always lived with animals and taken a keen interest in wild life. She started writing at a very early age and is now the author of bestselling novels, mainly based on her own experiences with animals; and of an equal number of children's books, one of which, *Jason*, has been filmed by Disney. *A Dog in a Million* is the latest book about her own dogs and follows the highly successful *Three's A Pack* and *Two for Joy*.

Joyce Stranger and her husband live in a 300-year-old cottage in Anglesey. They have three children, one an electronics engineer, one a vet and one a zoologist; and they have five grandchildren and four step-grandchildren.

Also by Joyce Stranger

and published by Corgi Books

A Dog in a Million

Joyce Stranger

CORGI BOOKS

A DOG IN A MILLION

A CORGI BOOK 0 552 12729 9

Originally published in Great Britain
by Michael Joseph Ltd.

PRINTING HISTORY
Michael Joseph edition published 1984
Corgi edition published 1986

This book is set in 11/12pt Bembo

Corgi Books are published by Transworld Publishers Ltd.,
61-63 Uxbridge Road, Ealing, London W5 5SA.,
in Australia by Transworld Publishers (Aust.) Pty. Ltd.,
15-23 Helles Avenue, Moorebank, NSW 2170, and in New
Zealand by Transworld Publishers (N.Z.) Ltd., Cnr. Moselle
and Waipareira Avenues, Henderson, Auckland.

Made and printed in Great Britain by
Hunt Barnard Printing Ltd., Aylesbury, Bucks.

Dedicated to Wendy Pyett, whose dogs make me laugh and whose letters are a delight.

And to all those like Wendy and myself, everywhere, who turn out, rain or fine, hot or cold, to run dog clubs all over the United Kingdom to help others, hopefully, to enjoy their dogs as much as we enjoy ours.

I hope those who read this book will appreciate you more!

CHAPTER ONE

She's a dog in a million, they said.

You'll never meet her like again, they said.

You'll never train *that*, they said.

What a challenge, they said.

Put it down, they said. Get a dog that is trainable.

I had a bitch like that, said my farmer neighbour. Trained her for sheepdog trials. I could always rely on her for just one thing.

What's that? I said.

To let me down when I most needed her co-operation. You won't train *that*, he said.

It was 1977 and they were all talking about my latest acquisition, Chita, a German Shepherd bitch puppy. I had already had two dogs with problems, I couldn't have a third, could I?

I could and did.

They didn't give me beauty when they were doling out the gifts for a child; but somehow they did give me a determination to *show* everyone. Tell me I *can't* and I *will*.

It probably stems from my father. He also wrote books, on wireless, before the days of transistors. One of his books starts 'There is no such word as *can't*, and another 'The impossible just takes a little longer'.

If ever I said 'I can't do it,' to him, he promptly said, 'Rubbish. Of course you can.'

They laughed at me at school when I said I wanted to write. My father didn't. He just knew that one day I would write. I don't know if any of those who laughed will ever know I have now written more than fifty books and proved them wrong. It no longer matters, but it did when I began.

They laughed at me when I said I wanted to train dogs. How daft can you get? Now I run a dog club and I train my own dog to compete against police dogs. I had a long battle to learn how to control her, as she is faster than any dog I have ever met, and full of energy which must be channelled into using her brain for our good, and not for mayhem. She is now six years old and we can get full marks in some of the Working Trials tests. They are advanced tests and it is long and demanding work to train a dog to excel at them. I am getting results with the dog in a million they said I'd never train.

The first two books on her produced so many letters from people with dogs similar to her, who had taken hope from my experiences, that this is to encourage them even more, and not to brag, as six years later she is a dog in a million in quite a different way.

Get rid of *that*, they had said, seven years before I bought Chita, looking at Janus, my semi-crippled Golden Retriever, who has bad hips. He won't live two years, they said, when they discovered he also had a dud pancreas and can't digest meat. That was twelve years ago. He is now thirteen, and last week chased a rabbit (well, he tried; an old dog hasn't that turn of speed, but Janus, like me, has always been determined to prove people wrong.) Exercise and care got over the crippling and the pancreas trouble too, though several kind souls who jumped to conclusions and didn't ask questions (they knew it all) tried to report me for neglecting my dog.

Dogs with pancreas trouble, until it is sorted, are desperately thin. Food goes through them at an amazing rate and is not digested. A year later I was competing with him in Obedience and he managed to get himself placed. He was thought untrainable too.

He was an impossible dog; a dog that wouldn't listen; a dog that never came when called, a dog that always did his own thing, and that was always something I did *not* want him to do. Like making friends with the judge in the ring, instead of walking to heel.

At one show, in the heel exercise without a lead, he weaved in and out of the poles that held the ring ropes, with a grin on his face, knowing I wasn't allowed to touch him, not listening to my voice, making the crowd laugh, but losing me most of our points.

I learned to laugh with him, and not to be upset when we made yet another boob in the ring. He is a character and a half, and has been a delight to live with and who can ask more than that?

Talk to some of the people who knew me at my first club and they will say with scorn, 'Oh Janus!'

He was wild; pulled like a maniac on the lead, raced after other dogs, and the only thing that calmed him was my hands on his body, holding him, and, I thought, he also responded to my soothing voice. Then Chita was tested to see if she were gun-shy when Janus was seven years old. She wasn't. Janus didn't hear the gun; not even when fired right behind him.

My impossible dog wasn't wild; he was *deaf* and, with that knowledge, everything slipped into place and I began to train with my hands on his head to make him watch me, and to use signals instead of words. We had no trouble after that at all. He is a super dog, but sadly, you can't compete with a deaf dog. It is against the Kennel Club rules. He did enter an Exemption show two years ago, beating much younger dogs, his head up, his tail waving, the old warrior come out for an airing, pride in every inch of his body.

He was two when I bought Puma, my first German Shepherd. She was seventeen months old when I brought her home. At five months she had had lead poisoning through licking paint, and they said I wouldn't train her either; lead poisoning destroys learning ability. She was trained, though it was a long hard slow slog, and she won two third prizes at Obedience when she was seven years old. I didn't ask for more; she went on in Breed shows and won a Championship Certificate and then she went blind.

No, this isn't a hard luck story!

Bad luck is only bad luck if you let it be. I've learned so much by having to train a deaf dog; I learned so much with my gentle, affectionate, but very anxious and slow to learn bitch. I had been helped with her, oddly enough, because I had once tamed a little wild hawk and had learned from that how to cope with a terrified creature, and she was far from terrified, only desperately anxious to do right, and finding humans so hard to understand.

Then I bought Chita. She was as wild as Janus had been, and far less biddable. She wanted her own way, always. She charged, at nine weeks old, down the pipe that led to the septic tank, as we had workmen here for her first two years. She was rescued, but resented it. She adored the concrete mixer; she also adored newlaid concrete. She dug under the fence at the top of the bank and slid through and hung by her collar, choking, while I tried to balance on piled-up stones and release her. She chewed my typewriter knob. She managed to maroon herself on the mantelpiece, screaming for help, (she still screams if she needs people to help her). She had to be put in a big playpen near me by day or she chewed electric flexes, and one thing she would not learn was the word NO.

A friend of mine wrote at the end of that first traumatic year: 'Please can you let me know sometime how you worked the miracle (on Chita) as we get problem dogs in club, though I am glad to say we have yet to have one as bad as Chita.' We had stayed with her twice. The first visit had been memorable: Chita went for both the family dogs and had to be kept separate.

I went to Edith Nicholls, who at that time ran the Garreg Ddu Academy. They have since moved away from the area. She wrote:

> Our introduction to Chita was so distasteful that Bob (her husband) and I agreed that it was highly likely that she would have to be put down. Here was Joyce Stranger desperately clinging to a lungeing, screaming, snappy bitch which within twenty minutes produced an extremely exhausted handler.
>
> We had a word with her and found her feelings were very mixed. She had obviously tried very hard to train her and spent many hours from each hard-working week in a desperate attempt to socialise her and teach her manners when away from home.
>
> For many years she had wanted a dog for Trials; she was disappointed with Chita, and yet for all her faults, loved her dearly and no way did she want to give up.

Edith and Bob are very good with hard temperament problem dogs, and without their help Chita would never have lasted. I got her under control; I began to compete in Trials though not often as all are far away and I am too busy, but she did make progress.

I hadn't realised then that my three problem dogs had given me an outstanding advantage over many other people. Deafness, blindness, lead poisoning, and now I have also learned from this little villain that, six years later, is a reformed character, that enchants everyone who gets to know her.

My vet discovered I trained my dog to a high standard for Trials. He suggested I started a dog club. I didn't want the responsibility; no salary and a major commitment, as dogs have problems in between club nights as well as on club nights. No way, I said.

But desperate people rang me up and came to the house and my time was eroded. I work in the mornings from 9 till 1; I train my dog in the afternoon and research my books then; I can't write about things I have never done.

I needed my private time. I discovered I could have a room in the Community Centre, and train people on one night a week. The City Council would back me (but not pay me). I didn't feel capable; I had so much to learn.

I began, sure it would fold up. I had not imagined the problems that come with dogs; the sad tales that can arise; the small tragedies; the heartbreak. If you run a dog club you become a confidante; a shoulder to cry on when a dog is put to sleep, but you also become a partner in an enterprise that often ends with a well trained dog. It's a delight to walk down the street and see one of my class in front of me, the dog perfectly behaved, the owner proud of the animal pacing at her or his side.

Why do it, and especially for nothing, people say. You must be mad, they say. How little they know.

Recently I was helping with a German Shepherd bitch as her owner has been ill. A delightful six-month-old, sweet and biddable. I got progress, and came home, and on the way remembered Chita at that age. I think it was only then that I realised what I had lived through with her. If she had been as easy as the one I was training that afternoon how different my life would have been.

And how much knowledge I would have missed. Also, I changed as I couldn't change my dog. Chita has made me tougher, more self-reliant, more confident. I have met hundreds of dogs in past years, and whatever others say, I know that my dog is nothing like any of them. Chita was really hard going. My struggles with her have made me more sympathetic with those who have problems. They have made me faster in my own reactions; have made me think and think again about club dogs and their problems and because my last three dogs were so very different, I know that every dog in club needs individual teaching.

If I hadn't kept Chita I would have missed hours of interest, hours of enthralment, hours of pleasure; with her and with my club dogs. The club now is forty strong, and people are progressing far better than before. I have learned far more.

But I will *never* know enough. We add to our breeds. Recently we added a Keeshond pup, and a Bull Terrier pup, which makes twenty different breeds now. Every dog is different; every breed is different. You can't train any two exactly alike.

I never know what is coming through the door.

There is endless fascination all the time, and as Chita progresses, even if we never get to the top, we have had fun trying.

It's very good for the soul and keeps my feet on the ground; if she won easily I might soar to the heights and never come down and be a very unpleasant person.

As it is I have the deepest sympathy for all the also-rans. I started the Society of Also-Rans; it's a joke and has very few members, but we all have the same problem with our dogs; they do so well in 70 per cent of the tests and let us down in the other 30 per cent. I once had 79 per cent in the lowest stake of Working Trials with Chita; if she had done the last two exercises, the stays, correctly, we'd have had 99 per cent. Only she didn't! So we couldn't qualify as we needed those marks; it's one exercise no dog may fail and still go on to qualify.

I'm not alone. There are dozens of us, all trying very hard, all never quite getting there. It is very far from easy.

It doesn't break my heart; a writer learns to take the rough with the smooth, the good reviews with the bad, and some of them can be awful. The worst now make me laugh. Especially if someone tries to compare me with authors who don't write my sort of books. Their readers wouldn't read mine anyway. I don't read theirs − we all prefer our own fields.

It's the same with dogs. If you have an easy dog or you win easily in shows you may scorn those who don't manage to win; never knowing the hills they have climbed, and the heights they have scaled, and the hours they have spent trying to get results, and the days they have suffered misery because the dog seemed impossible, the progress seemed minimal, the goal too far away.

This book is about Chita; my impossible dog; the untrainable dog; the dog that people now look at and simply believe I am lying, to make out I have achieved more than I have. It is also about the dogs that have been helped because of all I learned through her. Others can write about how they trained their dogs and won; but there are so many more concerned with controlling a difficult dog. I can help those with boisterous dogs and when someone comes to club as someone did recently, and tells me they think I ought to get rid of her, I can answer with confidence, 'Then we are going to prove them wrong, aren't we?' and set my heart and wits to finding out how to get on top of yet another energetic animal.

The trouble with these is that often they are far more devoted in their good moments than any of the easy dogs; they have so much character, and once you have shown them you are the boss, they change in nature and become a companion of a type that few people ever know.

I have never regretted my pup; even on my worst days with her, I have been glad I have her.

When I am tired, and it's been a long evening and progress has seemed minimal, I say that I will give up the dog club, and have my life to myself again, and then I go next week and the pups rush to greet me and a dog I didn't think would show progress has improved in a great leap and someone stops as I am packing up to go home and says 'I can't thank you enough,' and I know that I will never be able to give it up.

If we don't have club I miss it; there's something wrong with the week. If I can't get out to train Chita I feel the day lacks purpose; I watch her doing a long sendaway down the field to drop when I tell her, see her purposeful little body and her air of pride, or reward her with her stick (being Chita she needs a branch, not a stick) and see her carry it with immense poise, every inch of her saying watch me, aren't I *clever?* I savour her, every moment with her.

She's a star and I can't yet match her, or teach her well enough; her failure is not her own; it is mine because I lack the training that would have made her a champion. I am what some of the winning people call a Never Wuzzer.

I don't feel like that. A lot of it is luck; I live in the wrong place; have never been able to go to the best teachers. The dogs may win at Crufts, but *who* taught their owners? As for me, I think I always want another rung to climb, another book to write, another attempt at improving the dog I have; another dog, one day, to train.

Life is over when you have nothing left to achieve.

My goal is always just beyond my reach.

CHAPTER TWO

Much of my early unhappiness with Chita was due to the fact that I was spending my training time with Obedience people and not with Trials competitors.

I did not realise that for several years. Obedience training is rigid; the requirements are for a fast accurate dog that behaves almost like a robot. Many people love watching the dogs put through their paces, seeing each dog enter the ring and perform at heel, moving so accurately that very few can ever achieve that goal.

People with their eyes on winning prizes looked at my pup with scorn. Get rid of her and buy an easy dog. It was said over and over, until I began to have bitten lips through stifling extremely rude retorts. I was brought up to be polite and it's sometimes a big drawback!

I am never happy about the training necessary to get dogs to top standard. Those that enjoy it, fine, but if the owner is determined to get an also-ran dog to the top, then life for that dog is going to be misery as it is not capable of the accuracy and has to be forced. That may succeed; it certainly accounts for some of the cowed miserable dogs one sees in competition rings. 'OK, I'll do it as you'll be angry if I don't, but at a snail pace, with head hanging down and a defeated expression all over me.'

That is the last thing I ever want to see in my club.

I have always enjoyed watching dogs that are police trained. I used to go to the Police Trials at Bellevue when they were held in public. I remember, long ago, in the early 1960s, watching a big police dog handler with a superb white German Shepherd. You didn't see the signals; man and dog dog were so welded into their teamwork that the dog obeyed almost the flick of an eyelid. It was wonderful.

The majority of clubs teach Obedience work. This becomes very stereotyped. Owners learn to keep their dogs to heel, get straight sits, retrieve a dumbbell accurately and maybe go on to some more advanced exercises. If the dog sits crooked you are told you will lose points under a judge. But few pet owners are ever going to go under any judge. Few people who compete seem to realise the exercises are not aimed, in the first instance, at performing under a judge.

They are aimed at controlling the dog.

The dog does as it is told in all circumstances. If I have a class of twelve dogs in my room, and the caretaker races in and says 'The end room is on fire', I want every owner to be able to walk calmly out at a brisk pace, dog obeying on the instant, at heel, not tripping anyone up, and when outside, dogs to sit quietly beside their owners until we are told it is safe to go back, or that we must now take the dogs to the cars and go home.

While the dogs are waiting for their class to begin I expect them to lie calmly, without sniffing, playing, or barking. I never allow barking in club. It may take three weeks to cure it, but we have never yet had a failure in that. The owners must persist at home, of course. It is useless training a dog once a week; it has to be trained for living, so that everything it does during the day is acceptable to the family and the neighbours. They have rights too. It is pointless going to a dog club every few weeks, and idling in between. You and your dog, if you don't work at home and don't come regularly every week without fail, are a major nuisance as you never progress and you spoil the training for those who do come each week and do work hard. The hard truth is that that type of owner shouldn't really have a dog, as dogs do need teaching to behave, as children do.

Many dogs are easy and biddable; mostly those that come to club are the working breeds that need to be cured of bad habits and taught good ones. The training is like the alphabet; if you come for ABC, and then don't come back till the class has got to LMN, your dog will never train at all and you waste your money and the instructor's time.

Often a class may be organised to help a dog with major problems and after spending time and thought on working out a way to overcome them, you go down to take the class, and find the one owner you had geared everything around is missing. It means that you give up on that person as they aren't reliable enough to bother with. We ask for a term's fees in advance as a result of that, so we rarely have that problem now.

Although I never did much good in the competition ring with Puma, I could rely on her to behave herself in all kinds of circumstances. We went to Crufts, after we moved to Wales, by train, the year she won her Challenge Certificate. That is the highest award a dog can win at a Championship show, other than Best of Breed, which she also won that year, 1977, and Best in Show, which she didn't win. She sat beside me waiting for the train. She lay on her rug under the table all the way to London (it's a five-hour journey). She sat beside me waiting for a taxi. The taxi driver didn't like 'Alsatians'. (The German Shepherd is the correct name for the Alsatian. They are not two different breeds.) I assured him she would behave. I put down the little rug my mother had crocheted for her to travel on (it folded easily into a bag) and she didn't move throughout the journey. He changed his mind, at least about her. He also made a detour to take us to the park, waited for us, and didn't charge me for that part of the ride.

On our way home the train was delayed because someone had said there was a bomb on it. We had to get out at Crewe and wait while the train was taken away and searched. (It was a hoax call.) She came out quietly, heeled beside me down the platform and tucked herself up to sleep again while we waited for over an hour. A man standing near me said: 'I hate dogs, and I hate that breed in particular, but if they all behaved like yours, I could be converted.'

We arrived late, almost midnight, to an iced-up car and she sat quietly while I got it open (by breathing hard down the keyhole) and then got out the de-icing fluid, and coped. She jumped in when told and went to sleep again, for the fifteen-mile journey home.

That, to me, is what training is about. Not rosettes and cups and prizes; they are the icing on the cake. Lovely if you can win them, but the dog is much more important. Though if it comes to choosing between a human life and a dog's life, then the dog must come second.

Puma in her old age changed character and became likely to attack people; she had brain damage. The choice is hard, but I couldn't keep a dog that might damage someone badly. She was blind and confused by then; but still very sweet with me, and the decision was bitter, but the safety of my family and friends was my first consideration, and a dog that had already bitten once was a major liability.

That was a black day.

I had therefore to think very hard about Chita. She was not safe with other dogs, but she had to be safe with people. She now adores them, especially if they reciprocate. She is now safe with dogs under control, but if dogs are off-lead, running free, and rush at her and bark, she will see them off if she too is free. She doesn't attack, and she is unlikely to do more than bark. People tend to object, but then I object to having a strange dog rush up at us when she is walking quietly beside me, doing nothing wrong. My dog and I have rights, too!

I soon realised that I had a working dog; not a pet dog. These dogs are all the same; bred from stock that has ancestors that worked, whether guard dogs, or gundogs. They are workaholics, extremely alive, very energetic and with a driving need to *work*, whether it is retrieving birds, or protecting property and people. The only way to get any sense into a pup like this is to behave like a gundog man, or a policeman...or get rid of it.

So many people buy dogs advertised as from police dog breeding; they are wonderful...for policemen. Or farm Collies, which are marvellous, so long as you have sheep; or gundogs from a gamekeeper; super, if you shoot. Jack Russells from a farmer or a gamekeeper will, as a rule, be great ratters; they won't be biddable hearthrug pets.

So many people complain their Retrievers pick things up and won't let go. Of course they won't; they were bred to retrieve pheasants. So every Retriever puppy needs his 'pheasant'. Janus's is a dilapidated old fur glove and if I forget his glove he strips my right-hand glove off and carries that; I can put my hand in my pocket to keep warm, so there!

So with Chita I had to do the same; not pretend to have shot a pheasant and let her carry it home, or bring it to me, but as she was a guarding breed, to be a pretend policeman, or give my dog up altogether. It was a challenge; and I like challenges, and with the memory of that long-ago police-dog team in mind, I knew where I wanted to go.

Working Trials training is based on police dog work, without the manwork. The dog is taught to track; very sensible as if you get lost, or a member of your family does, then the dog has a very useful skill. Chita has several times guided me back to the car through the woods or the dunes, retracing our original path.

The dog is taught to search for small articles hidden in the grass. The police dog is looking for murder clues, or evidence left after a robbery, and hunts for any article bearing human scent. The pet dog becomes a finder of lost articles. Chita has found my gloves, and my wedding ring, and Janus found a hotel key I had dropped in a huge field in long grass behind the hotel when I exercised the dogs. I felt very silly as we had only just arrived. My dog saved me having to confess that I had lost their key!

The dog is taught to walk at heel beside you and sit when you halt; not an accurate military walk but a sensible position, out for a walk, keep by master's side, and don't run off. Very useful if there are several dogs with you, and all can be kept under control in that way. Very difficult to teach when dogs belonging to other people run up and interfere with your training, as they often do.

The dog is also taught to run a hundred yards away from you in a straight line at a fast pace and drop down. The police use this as an interception exercise; a man is running along behind a wall and the dog is sent to a gap ahead of him and is there before him and the arrest is made. In our lives it is very useful as if the dog races out to chase a child or another dog or a cat or a sheep, a call of *down* drops the dog; you can then go and put the lead on and prevent a problem developing. You have practised dropping the dog when running at full speed in order to perfect the sendaway exercise.

If we were on the dunes and Puma saw a car moving in the distance she was always triggered to chase, before she went blind, but she dropped at once, so that I never had a real problem. I did have to watch her, though.

I knew what I wanted from Chita.

The trouble was that there was no one at all who knew how to teach me, as everyone was Obedience orientated, and though I didn't realise it then so much as I do now, that was not what either Chita or I needed. Also they were intensely critical of my wild dog and her behaviour, and they did not know that the Trials training is very different, in its approach, to the rigid disciplines of Obedience, and that if they were ever to do Trials, they would have to start learning all over again. I didn't know that then, either.

In fact I now think it likely that the Trials approach would be a far happier one for most Obedience dogs, and would get better results with many of the dogs that aren't geared to highpowered Obedience work. Most of those that win these days are bred for the job; the Crufts lists have relatively few names of Kennels in them; the top dogs all tend to come from the same sources. Breeding counts for so much in every field of work with dogs. Trials training is much more relaxed, and far easier for dogs that are not deliberately bred to excel at the Obedience routines.

My first feelings about Chita, due to the insistence of everyone around me (silly how you judge yourself at times by what other people say! Good job I don't believe some reviewers!) were that I was to blame for her wildness.

Then I began to use my wits.

I had had several years of walking Puma and others from her Kennels, then at Mobberley in Cheshire, as Judy Pillings showed her Gorsefields, and when I took Puma out to get her show fit, I often took three other German Shepherds, all fully grown and mostly male, with her. I was used to walking four German Shepherds at a time for a five-mile walk without any problems and now I couldn't walk one small pup; she was a maniac!

But I had a well-behaved Golden Retriever and an immaculately behaved adult German Shepherd, so it could not be *my* fault. None of my past dogs had been difficult — they were all very biddable so it had never occurred to me to take them to a dog club.

I could give up, but that is silly. Be defeated by one small animal?

When I buy a dog it is for life. I took it on; it didn't ask me to. Why should I put it down because it doesn't win me prizes and feed my ego. I want success for my dog if I can give it to her and she is able to do it; not to boost myself through her. Whether I qualify her or not, Chita has me hooked. No other dog will ever be as alive as Chita; no other dog will ever make me feel so sure that I can manage other dogs, as mostly I can and do manage her. She lets me down, yes, but if she weren't trained, boy, would people stare. She wouldn't be alive, that's for sure.

Bev Telfer from New Zealand confirmed that for me this summer when she came for the day, during a holiday in Britain. She owns a dog that is closely related to Chita. She had read *Three's A Pack,* the first book about my imp. We spent a heavenly afternoon talking dogs and talking about Chita and about Bev's Chita cousin, and our problems with them. She knew what I went through, and still at times suffer through my little wretch. She has endured many such incidents.

Only the day before Bev's visit, after years of training, I let Chita out on the field. Our cottage is in the middle of a field. It isn't a grand cottage; it's a weird one; it started about 1700 as two rooms and has been added on to until we need a dog to guide us up to bed! Visitors call out 'Where am I?' as they face about five doors. Part of it is stone and very warm; part is modern and very cold and the central heating, which is oil-fired as there is no gas here, works as long as it isn't blowing a gale. Recently Kenneth designed a weird extra indoor gadget to see if that would help control the draught and keep us warm on windy days. So far it's working, but it looks quite extraordinary, which is the story of a lot of the built-on bits of this house.

Three hundred and fifty nine days a year there isn't a problem when I let Chita out. About six days a year there is a stray cat. If I see it, fine, I say NO, and she comes to me. Yesterday I didn't see it; it was in the long grass, lurking, as Chita went out of the door (I had double checked; you always double check with a dog like Chita).

The cat flew, and Chita flew, I yelled NO and I yelled DOWN and I yelled COME and then gave up as both had disappeared; I charged at top speed up the three-hundred-yard, one-in-five slope to the gate, cursing. The cat vanished; and next door to me opposite the disused and derelict quarry is the sheep field; with a gate that is easily leaped by a dog that had already leaped a similar gate. Just as I was prepared to hear mayhem from the sheep next door, Chita appeared in the lane, tail waving, a grin on her face, and sat at our gate, on the wrong side. Angelic animal, waiting for me to open the gate and let her in. Couldn't jump it now, could she, hadn't really jumped it at all, hadn't a clue how she'd got the wrong side of it, had she?

Good girl, aren't I? Come back, haven't I? and there is no way she can be punished because she *has* come back and if I did punish her, next time she wouldn't bother; why come back to someone who thumps you on arrival for something you have already forgotten you have done? Been thumped for coming back to her; next time I won't. Not that she ever gets thumped. That's no way to train a dog.

The dog that won't return has usually been accidentally given the wrong message; the dog lives *now*. The past vanishes, except for longstanding associations like walk, lead; and bowl, food. Those happen so often and are repeated so often he does remember.

The people who have easy dogs are so scornful of this chasing behaviour and so critical that I mentioned it, a little forlornly, when I rang one of the men I knew who has qualified several dogs in Working Trials.

He reassured me. He had been up in Scotland with his fully trained highly qualified German Shepherd, when the dog saw a cat run, while they were out walking, and took off. He didn't come back till the cat vanished under a gate.

'We are training animals, Joyce,' he said. 'We can't take away their instincts and if they are a few yards away from you when a hare or a rabbit or cat starts up there is no way whatever the best handler in the world can get that dog back. Don't expect so much; it wasn't you. Chita is only a *dog*.' I've since met a police dog and a Guide Dog that, when off duty, can never resist chasing cats.

Every dog I know pales into insignificance beside Chita. If my next one is too placid I will be bored beyond belief as she is a handful, all the time; she is a challenge, all the time; and the more I know about her, the more I learn about her, the better I learn to control her, the more fascinated I become by the sheer complexity of dog behaviour, by owning a dog in a million, a kind of dog few other people are lucky enough to have.

Though maybe they wouldn't regard it as luck and would put her down. They prefer life easy.

Now I am often among people who like rough tough dogs I feel much happier. My police dog handler friends tend to like the sort of dogs that rush around with builders' planks in their mouths. Eric

Roberts, who has helped me a great deal, was the first instructor I have ever had who approved wholeheartedly of Chita and thinks her a terrific bitch. The last thing he would ever suggest is putting a dog down unless it was mental; he likes to get them rough and get them under control and many a wild dog, now tamed, owes its existence to him today.

His methods are quite different to any I had ever been taught. Although Eric is a professional he is addicted to dogs and once said that it seems absurd to be paid for doing something he enjoys so much. Even manwork is taught there differently. I don't approve of the way some people teach it, but this is something else, the way the best police forces teach it, very carefully, so that the dog is under total control and can be trusted to find a lost child or an old person who has lost their memory, as safely as to track down or chase a crook.

It makes a great deal of difference to work on Chita when I know that what she is doing is acceptable and her tremendous energy and ability to make mistakes is considered an asset to be used. I have to work with it, not crush it out of her.

I know now that a lot of the times when people say she is mucking me about, or is being disobedient, she is not. She is confused. She is an intelligent dog and jumps to conclusions, often wrongly. Picking the lead up doesn't always mean a walk; it may mean it's in the wrong place, but she is by the door, eager, waiting. Picking her bowl up doesn't invariably mean food; it may mean that it is in the wrong place, and she watches and then as I put it away without filling it, her whole body droops. Was wrong again, wasn't I? Eric's comment is that she isn't a pet dog, she is a dog handler's dog, the sort a real handler likes, presenting problems above the average dog. Only an expert handler could help me, and he is the first instructor I have ever had with Chita who is a good handler and has a passion for dogs.

He is a very good instructor, able to put over what he wants, and never guilty of the type of comment that makes his pupil feel diminished or destroys confidence. He is critical but never destructively so; he always has a suggestion to make to improve on what you are doing, and his methods of teaching have helped me become a better teacher too.

One day we were teaching Chita the long sendaway. She has to run up to a hundred yards or more and drop on my command. For years she found it very difficult to understand. I thought she was defiant; she wasn't; she was confused. Eric pointed out that it isn't the setup at the beginning that matters, it is *where* the dog goes; all the praise has to come when she reaches her goal, and till she understands the exercise no amount of setting her up and pointing is going to teach it to her. She will sit there like an angel, pointed in the right direction but what makes her *go*?

After two lessons of about half an hour each she got the idea and off she trotted, right down the field. I was about to follow her when Eric caught my arm.

'Don't,' he said. 'Stand and enjoy it. You'll never have the satisfaction of a moment like this again. The first time. She has the idea, is doing it right and doing it perfectly. Savour it.'

I did and it taught me so much more because now each small step forward is an achievement and each time she does as I ask I remember that day and those words, and I stand and savour her. Clever dog.

My dog in a million.

She bangs her muzzle at my knee. No gentle nudge with Chita.

Let's go.

Let's go anywhere, but let's be doing. No more sitting and writing; come on, let's be out.

Walking bores me; it seems pointless, going

nowhere to come back again, but out in the fields I know heaven, alone with my dog, under the trees, teaching her, watching her, enjoying her. Every second with her. It reminds me daily of the thrill I felt many years ago when the hawk I had tamed so patiently for days flew on his line towards me and fed from my hand, coming of his own free will, trusting me. The wild bird tamed.

I was talking on the phone recently to a friend who trains police dogs. He has just lost his last dog at six years old through a hip complaint and has had several since. He is hoping his new young dog will be a success.

He said:

'Joyce, how do we tell people who only have a dog in the house as a pet and take it for a walk, just what they are missing? Out there with the dog, finding the track, watching it search, teaching it so much, more every day, and having it respond. How can we make them see?'

We can't and never will. Even some who compete for prizes may not really ever know what we achieve with our dogs; what we feel for our dogs, how we work with our dogs. There are dozens of us, many like myself running dog clubs and not getting far because when we ought to be working with our own dog, we are helping someone who has a problem that was once ours; a dog out of control; a dog that might be put down because it has chased sheep; a dog giving its owner immense worries because of its brashness.

Our achievement comes when that dog too is under control. As I stand and watch the dogs from club file out, on lead, none pulling, none barking, and see them walk off into the night after club, I know how lucky I am. I can't tell other people; very few would understand that, to me, to help someone train a Yorkie to behave is just as rewarding as to help someone else train a dog of the guard dog breeds up to a high standard, or take my own to the top.

I won't get to the top with Chita and may never with another dog.

I will have the knowledge that through me a number of people who might have given up on their dogs have kept them, trained them and now enjoy them instead of wishing they had no dog.

CHAPTER THREE

The first book on Chita (*Three's A Pack*) describes her mad puppy days; they were mad too! Mostly I found her hilarious but as few others did, I was always conscious of a need to make her behave like the kind of dog she isn't, the placid meek biddable dog.

When I wrote about her, people often thought I was complaining bitterly; probably putting into my mind the thoughts they would have had about her! I was usually laughing!

In the second book (*Two for Joy*) she was nearly four; and much more easily controlled. She led me into all sorts of extraordinary byways as I sought for ways of getting her under better control, getting her to accept other dogs without attacking them, and then getting her up to a good Trials standard.

I have travelled some odd but fascinating byways through owning a dog like Chita; as through her I have met so many people, and through her have made my best friends.

My friendship with Wendy Pyett started in the daftest way. I had read her very entertaining articles in *Dog Training Weekly*. She owned two dogs when I first read her hilarious accounts of living with Ross. She now owns three. Ross is also a German Shepherd, and Ross has Puma's sense of humour, a sense of humour I now miss – Puma did so love a joke. Wendy, whose birthday is the day before mine, thinks so like me that writing to her is a bit like writing to myself, and I know that if I think something is funny she will too.

We haven't met, but she was aware of me through my articles in the same publication, as we both write for the same dog papers. We also both take *The Shepherd Dog* which is published by the British Association for German Shepherd Dogs. Wendy competes in agility; I compete in Trials; we both teach in dog club; we are both hooked on German Shepherds; and we both own dogs that are quite a handful. Mostly we both laugh at their misdeeds which are not too awful but we both have to exert real authority at times in a way that people with little dogs would never understand (and I *don't* mean by brutality!).

The Shepherd Dog is a quarterly publication.

One quarter I noticed that Wendy had started an agony column for dogs, purporting to be by Ross! He wrote again in the next issue, but seemed not to have any dogs with problems, so Chita wrote to him, telling him how she had had to do a downstay on an anthill and had been bitten, as had all the other dogs.

It had been in the forest and all the dogs came up with lumps on their tummies; one dog was badly bitten in the most vulnerable place for the male, and swelled so alarmingly he had to be rushed to the vet.

Ross commented that he was very embarrassed by being asked about ants in a lady's pants and suggested that the dogs asked their handlers to sit where they were to lie down in future, and perhaps we would be more careful. I have never met ants before like this at Trials, so perhaps we can be forgiven; I now inspect the ground she is to lie on!

My letter was too long to publish in its entirety so the editor sent it on to Wendy. A few days later Chita had a letter from Ross; this correspondence was so funny that both of us kept it up; it was silly, amusing, relaxing and it did have the virtue of making us see things from our dogs' viewpoint and help us in understanding our dogs and other dogs much better. We both had two dogs when the correspondence started.

Both dogs are quite convinced their owners have the most peculiar and unreasonable views; every self-respecting dog knows sofas are to lie on, so why ban the poor dog when *we* sit on it? Also dogs only eat once a day; humans never stop. Since Wendy and I both try to diet, without much success, the dogs have a very useful way of reminding us that there is no need to snack as well as feed; we keep them lean and fit, and we ought to do the same for ourselves.

It is also hard to blame a dog for doing what dogs do naturally when we can't stop our supposedly much more reasonable selves from sampling that bar of chocolate we both know perfectly well we should not have bought anyway!

Ross wrote last Christmas to say that he was embarrassed to tell Chita he was about to be a dad and hoped she wasn't jealous. She wrote back to say: 'I don't mind a bit. I'm an It.' Now Wendy also owns Ross's daughter and is learning all over again that there is no easy road to a well-behaved dog. Ziena's latest exploit has been to tear up the carpet. She is about seven months old as I write.

The correspondence changed its nature last summer when Wendy's husband died suddenly of heart trouble and since then we have written reams to one another about our dogs, about dog club dogs, and about our lives in general. If it hadn't been for Chita this friendship would never have started and I would have missed a great deal of pleasure, as well as being able to increase my knowledge of dogs, as every deed and misdeed of every dog one knows adds to one's experience, and may help to bring yet another dog under control, and save it from either being given away or from the death chamber.

Chita has taught me so much more than any of my other dogs that I felt I ought to pass on the knowledge; it isn't book knowledge. Chita hasn't read the books and nor have any other dogs in club!

Dogs don't all behave alike, even from the same litter, from the same parents, or of the same breed. I am not in the least like either of my sisters. Dogs are no different. The same parents don't make them clones and the silliest exercise I have found is a repeat mating; the first may produce wonderful animals and the next nothing like them. Reproduction does not conform to a formula. People say it does but how on earth can it? If it did every member of each family would be exactly like the other members; even identical twins aren't always absolutely similar, though they come from a split egg.

I have two litter sisters in club now; both are German Shepherds. Their mother is one of the loveliest natured bitches we have ever had in club; one of her pups is so full of life she may well prove another Chita though she is far more biddable; the other is already beginning to show signs of sense, yet both come from the same litter.

Our two Dobe brothers differ in temperament and are totally different colours; you would never guess they came from the same parents. Jason, a very light brown, is a one-off at club, as the other Dobermanns from the same kennels are black and tan, like Jason's brother.

There is absolutely no rule in nature at all and those who are sure there is do need to think harder, and not be so rigid in their decrees!

I always remember Judy Pilling, Puma's breeder, ringing me up. She planned to breed Burmese cats and had a very attractive but rather self-willed queen named Black Secret.

'Come and see Secret's secret,' Judy said on the phone.

I drove over and looked in mild disbelief at a very happy little mother suckling four ginger and black kittens. Judy laughed.

'The best of plans. I don't even know where she met a ginger Tom!' Judy, like me, rarely expects life to be predictable.

Life can be very difficult, often in the most unexpected ways.

One of the most difficult things in dog club is that owners of dogs like Shelties are convinced their dogs behave like that because their owners are such good trainers, and the bouncy boisterous big dogs behave so badly (in the eyes of those with tiny easy dogs) because their owners are so totally unable to control them. It is easy to exert authority over an animal that only comes up to your calf, though some owners of little dogs have spoiled them to such an extent they aren't really fit to live with; they demand their own way and boss the family. Life is very different with an animal you can't pick up to avoid trouble, and whose head is level with your knee or thigh. This misunderstanding showed up remarkably when I once got into idiotic trouble with, of all people, the Tar Council!

When I lived in Cheshire I used to walk Puma and some of Judy's stock for a five-mile trip round Mobberley to keep them show fit. Walking on roads is far better for getting them fit than letting them run riot, as there is no risk of laming them by a careless twist of the body, or having them put a leg down a rabbit hole and tear a tendon.

I took out so many of them: Klaus who was hypersensitive; you could never raise your voice to him. Puma's brother Porky who died of lead poisoning. He was gorgeous. Panther, another brother. Witch, Puma's mother, and various others that have now been forgotten. I usually found four German Shepherds easier to cope with than one Janus. I hadn't then found out that he was deaf. Once I did, life became far easier.

On this occasion, while I was out for well over an hour, unknown to me, the local council resurfaced the road that lay between me and the cul-de-sac that led to the Kennels. There was no way I could get the dogs home except to walk over it.

I had Puma with me, and Janus and two of Judy's dogs. All adult; all weighing considerably over eighty pounds so I couldn't carry them. Reluctantly and worriedly, I did walk them across. Three of the dogs were fine, but Puma blistered her paws, and we had a great deal of trouble with them.

I wrote to one of the newspapers to warn people about this hazard and said the road had been tarred.

I got a furious letter from the tar manufacturers saying it couldn't have been tar, as that doesn't damage animals and can be used medicinally on farm animals. Had I tested it? It could have been asphalt, macadam, bitumen or any one of a number of things I had never heard of. I wrote to apologise and say I didn't carry a test kit with me, I didn't know there were different kinds of road surface, not being an expert, and whatever it was, it had blistered one dog's paws, though not the others. They wrote back to say something must have been spilt on the road.

It probably had. All I had wanted to do was to warn other dog owners to avoid newly surfaced roads if possible!

That wasn't the end of it as someone wrote to the paper to say anyone in her senses (which obviously didn't include me!) would have lifted the four dogs and carried them. I don't know if anyone has tried at five foot one and about eight stone seven to cart four dogs weighing nearly as much each over a road; I wasn't likely to do more than get to the middle and fall flat under my burden! I suppose I could have tied them up and fetched the car but knowing Puma she would have eaten through her lead and followed me.

She turned up once in the ring while I was working Janus, holding her bitten-through lead in her mouth and greeting me with enthusiasm. The judge said acidly: 'Can you make up your mind as to which dog you want?'

I gave her to a bystander to hold. I think the general feeling was I was rather incompetent, but people didn't know Puma. She once managed to let herself and Janus and three other dogs, one of which was a Crufts Champion, out of a paddock at the Guide Dog for the Blind Centre. They had put guide dogs in there for the lifetime of the paddock and never had any dog managed to open the dogproof gate before. I told them Puma would; they didn't believe me.

We had to change the catch on our front door because Puma would open the door and let all the dogs out. I had visions of my three creating mayhem in the sheepfield next door.

The lady who suggested that I carried the dogs across the road obviously had a tiny dog, no experience of large breeds, and their abilities, and hadn't stopped to think.

I always found I could understand mothers of sons and mothers of daughters as I had both, but families with only girls are very different to families with only boys! My daughter sails and caves and runs in marathons; she does also knit and sew, but her interests are not exclusively feminine.

Limited experiences limit understanding. Those owners who have only had dogs do not understand the problems of those with bitches. Puma was my first bitch and I found her positively alarming until I got used to her ways and her infuriating metabolism which insisted on seasons every seventeen weeks; which meant three weeks out of every four months she was unable to mix with other dogs.

Those who only have bitches don't know what it is like to own a lovelorn male that howls all night and won't eat because the bitch next door is in season and he can't have her.

Those with easy dogs tend to be very smug about

the problems of those whom they brand as incompetent with large dogs; they should find out what it feels like to own something the size of a Shetland pony!

One night in club I tried to show the owner of our only Rottweiler, a pup not yet six months old, how to get him to sit correctly. Spike is a huge fellow, a gorgeous dog, with a lovely nature, but he will sprawl. He must weigh as much as I do, and I found that I needed thigh, knee, elbow, foot and wall to get him where I wanted. He took it all with the greatest good humour. I wasn't using my strength to hurt him; just to cope with him. Whereas all I needed to do an hour later with our minute Yorkie was to slide her legs from under her and gently coax her to lie down. A very different matter! She must weigh about three pounds.

One thing about the owners of large dogs is that they are never smug!

Chita has also helped me to delve far more deeply into dog training, from sheer necessity, and the result is that I have to be careful when I teach to make sure I am not being too advanced for my class. My most rewarding conversations are with people like Eric Roberts, as he also trains advanced dogs, protection dogs, and competes in all the stakes at Trials including the Police Dog Stake; my police dog handler friend, who also takes dogs up to the highest possible standard; John Cree, who is extremely knowledgeable and a great help if I phone him; Roy Hunter also is full of good advice. All are very experienced trainers.

They make me think when we talk, and often make me see something from a different viewpoint. My police dog handler friend judges a great deal; especially Trials at police level, which are far stiffer than civilian trials. If I comment on a track being unusually difficult, he at once sees it from a working viewpoint; a police dog can't choose to track only in a nice clean field; villains don't make tracks that the dog can follow easily!

I find it difficult to talk to some who compete in Trials as they don't seem to think about the way a dog learns or the way a dog works; they take short cuts in training, and expect the dog to be telepathic and conform to an ideal they haven't even begun to train for in the right way.

There are many like myself and I begin to suspect we have a great advantage in teaching at pet club level as we are very well aware of the limitations of both dogs and owners. I want success for everyone, not just a favoured few, but it can tax my wits to work out how best to get it with one particular dog.

CHAPTER FOUR

Training a dog is very different from managing a dog. Those that are trained change in character, and become very rewarding to live with. Training develops the dog's intelligence, improves its personality and can prevent many harassing or even dangerous incidents.

These are not always avoidable. Few dogs will fail to retaliate if attacked, though Puma never did. She was bitten four times. Three of those bites happened when she was on the lead, just walking. All she did was squeal and come to me. One of the bites was severe. A stray dog, running free in the park, raced up to Puma, who was playing with Janus, off-lead, as I had not seen any other dogs near us. He apparently butted her in the side and ran off. She squealed.

I went to her and discovered he had, quite literally, taken a piece out of her side and left a hole. When I went to the vet, he described the dog and said that Puma was the fourth he had had in a fortnight. You never know what a dog will do if it is left free to wander. That episode cost me forty pounds in vet bills. After that, I insured against trouble, which has proved very worth while.

We had two club incidents last session. Spike, our Rottweiler, for reasons known only to himself, reached up, took the valve of the pressure cooker off the draining board and swallowed it. The operation cost the best part of a hundred pounds, but his owner had insured and so only had to pay the first £5 plus the VAT. Spike is now recovered and went home complete with the sterilised pressure-cooker valve.

Goldie's owner was less lucky. Goldie is a charming little Golden Retriever cross, and she took it into her head to start swallowing stones. She vomited two back but the third caused problems and Goldie had to have the stone removed. The insurance form, filled in, was waiting to be posted. That was an expensive exercise.

Both dogs had only begun training. It takes time even to teach a dog NO.

Although I have four instructor's certificates, of different grades up to advanced, theory doesn't help you train dogs. You need experience, and there is only one way to get that and that is to do it.

I hadn't realised how much my background experiences with wild animals and farm animals were going to help. I am used to helping herd sheep; sheep are very awkward sensitive creatures, easily panicked; so are some dogs.

If you watch sheepdog trials you will see the way the dog has to stalk, very cannily, never flurrying the sheep. A brash dog will send them all over the place. Approach one of our timid puppies by moving fast, and you panic the pup. So I approach it as I do a sheep; very cautiously. With a puppy, I make myself small, and sit on the floor and wait for him to come to me. I never rush at him and pick him up and make cooing noises at him. That is enough to terrify a dog that has never seen you before and is unfamiliar with your scent.

Hours of trying to coax fox and badger cubs to come to me have paid off, as, with the nervous pup, it may take several weeks to get him to overcome his fear of people, new places and other dogs that are much more bouncy and extrovert than he is. You can't start any real training until he has learned to relax with strange people, places and dogs. Fear prevents learning.

I like to take people slowly when they first join the club, as I have memories of going to a number of clubs where I simply didn't understand what I was being taught, why I was taught it, or how to get my dog to do it. People assumed you knew much more than you did, or else they were competing, and had no idea that the exercises were taught to dogs long before anyone dreamed up competitions. They simply taught them as they used to teach a child to learn by rote, without understanding what he is learning or why.

It is like learning the alphabet forwards and backwards, but never using it to put words together as nobody tells you why you learned it in the first place. Also experienced people rarely realise how very nervous a newcomer to club can be for the first few weeks.

I had one owner come last session with a very outgoing pup that wanted everyone to fuss him. That is almost more difficult than the shy pup. This dog is a very appealing little fellow and since he asks for petting he gets it, and that, quite simply, was spoiling him. He was becoming extremely silly.

He had to learn to listen to his owner and obey him. After four weeks I said: 'Your little dog is settling down nicely.' 'No,' was the reply, 'I'm the one that has settled down.' That little dog did extremely well when it came to the certificate test.

I like to keep classes small, so that I have four classes a night, of about ten people in each. I don't go over twelve. Our room is small and you need space for each dog, and you can't give the dogs individual attention with too many owners and dogs present.

I wished always when I first started in club that I could have more teaching of theory and how you applied exercises to living, but I was always taught how you applied them to being judged, which isn't the same thing at all.

I didn't progress with Janus until I had individual lessons from Audrey Wickham, now married to Edward Hart who writes books on country matters. She helped me enormously and led me on to competition with Janus.

It took years to get him to lie down sensibly; he was impossible, like many of his breed. He would go down on his front legs with his hind legs up and tail waving madly; he would lie on his back and bicycle or suck his paw. He would weave his paws round the lead and pull on it, or bat at my hand with one paw.

Golden Retrievers are gorgeous dogs but can be very stubborn. Also, they bore fast, so that any teaching has to be kept very short. They respond better if you play with them. So do all dogs. You have to learn how to control the play so that the dog doesn't overexcite and get out of hand; he might bite in sheer exuberance then.

I know now that Janus was an exceptionally difficult dog of his breed mostly because of his deafness. People said: 'He doesn't respect you. You must *make* him respect you.' They suggested all kinds of methods, like yelling at him, using a rolled-up magazine to hit him with, or a riding whip, or pinching his cheek or his ear.

Janus is a rough tough fellow. His idea of a game when in his heyday was to rush at Puma and send her spinning; she retaliated with glee. Short of picking him up and throwing him several yards, which is impossible, I doubted if any physical method that I could use, not being a strong navvy-type woman, would have the slightest effect and anyway, I didn't care for the advice.

My greatest help at this time was John Holmes's book, *The Family Dog*. He doesn't use those methods either.

At that time I felt people who ran dog clubs must be very much more experienced in every way than I was. I was wrong, as sometimes somebody has a dog for the first time for a couple of years, goes into competition and because it's an easy dog without problems, or is an exceptionally clever dog, they win. They then set up as experts. The next dog they get probably sorts them out, so they get rid of it, and keep on buying and selling dogs till they get another easy dog. They don't teach you how to train *your* dog; they teach you how they trained *their* dog. Since every dog is an individual that doesn't help you at all.

I train the dog I have, as I don't like the thought of another home that might not be a good one, and don't see why problems I may have caused in the dog by my lack of knowledge of *that* dog, should be handed on to anyone else. I don't like putting a healthy dog to sleep, but I would prefer that to rehousing it with total strangers. I come across too many unhappy dogs that have had to be rescued and come to club with new owners, who have taken on a really terrible task of rehabilitation. It can work. Often you can't get over the dog's past and he becomes a liability, attacking people who remind him of the owner who abused him.

One little dog always went for small fair women with glasses who wore a particular kind of hat. Another for men who looked like tramps with long flapping raincoats and beards.

How to earn a dog's respect? You can't train well till you have it. It wasn't till I found the American methods of training, which are based on the dog's mentality and the way bitches train their pups, that I saw any light at the end of this tunnel. A lot of people think the US methods absurd and are very scornful, but my feeling is that you don't condemn a method until you have tried it and found it fails.

I have found it works.

So that the first thing I explain in my club to new owners is that the dog is a pack animal and must have a leader. If he does not have a leader, he becomes pack leader; and a pack leader in the dog world may discipline those that don't do as he wants them to, with his teeth.

I didn't try the American method on Janus until he was nearly seven. I had not heard of it till then. By then he was willing to co-operate with me, but I had often had to battle with him. I had to battle with Chita.

Be fierce, they said. Be more dominant, they said. (How?) It is very hard when you are not a fierce large person to behave as if you were. You don't have the strength.

The silly thing is you don't need the strength. All you need is knowhow and determination.

The first thing your dog *must* learn is that you are the boss. He has to learn to submit. The submissive position is lying down, flat on the floor. An older dog runs up to a puppy, or a less dominant dog. The less dominant animal at once lies on his back and may leak a few drops of urine; that tells the older dog the puppy or the other dog is not going to fight him; so please leave it alone. Only a really bad dog will harm the pup after that.

If your dog lies down to greet you and lifts his leg for his tummy to be rubbed, he is a meek dog, and you won't have a lot of trouble in training unless he is so dozy he won't bother to try and work properly; he will be willing and want to do as you want. The dog that refuses to lie down and struggles violently is a pack leader.

There are dogs that use the down position as submission but also as a form of defiance in the hope that if they lie flat you will be induced *not* to insist that they do what you want. Dogs are very clever at manipulating their owners.

'Oh, poor dog. She's tired.' The dog has won, as the owner doesn't insist and the lesson is wasted.

If someone says: 'My dog doesn't like doing so-and-so,' and if so-and-so is desirable, and not doing it is not, then my reply is: 'I don't like washing up. Nobody lets me off that!'

Both Janus and Chita struggle on the down. Very frustrating at the time. Very useful as experience now. Puma went down like a lamb. She was very biddable and easy; my relaxing dog. The others could be headaches.

Now the first exercise I teach in club always is the down. In the new class that has just joined there are twelve dogs, aged from eight months to two years old, none of which has been trained at all.

Ten of them went down easily, once they understood what was wanted, by being shown by their owners, either by sliding their legs forward from a sitting position, or holding a toy or a titbit in the hand, which is placed on the floor (most dogs go down to take it) and saying DOWN as they did this, and then praising them.

This gives me my first clue to their future training, as all these are relatively easy. They are all big dogs. We have in that class four Labradors, all of them black, five German Shepherds, a Gordon Setter, a Springer Spaniel and a Boxer.

The Boxer is up to every trick Janus ever played on me and the Springer is like a yo-yo. Both are very nice dogs, but both are dominant and extremely wilful. Neither will begin to train until they learn their owners are stronger than they are as every step of the way will be a battle, and it's just not worth trying it that way; you don't win, the dog does and the whole relationship goes sour.

I can get both down; their owners can't. The instructor has a major advantage, as he or she not only bosses all those dogs, but all those owners. There you are telling owners what to do and they obey you, never mind the dogs; so the dog looks at you and thinks if you make his owner do what you want then, by golly, he'd better behave for you too. I can take several of our more fiendish dogs and get instant good behaviour; maybe if I put their owners in front of the class to teach for a while the dog might respect them more, but it's not easy to teach dogs and owners. People think it is; they are wrong!

For that matter it isn't easy to teach a dog until you have worked out what type of dog it is and even then it may do something you have never seen in your life before, or it may, out of the blue, react oddly.

Puma's refusal, suddenly, after months of success, to retrieve her dumbbell in the class or ring, was interpreted by my trainers and judges as a) stupidity b) obstinacy c) defiance. I knew it wasn't any of those and tried throwing it different distances. She was beginning to go blind and if it went beyond six feet she just couldn't see it; it had gone out of her range of vision. So it doesn't do to jump to conclusions. You need to think about each dog as an individual and try and work out just why something is happening.

The police are lucky. They get the dogs, sort out the temperaments, and then the fast-moving rather excitable type of man gets a slow dog that needs geeing up and making come alive, and the excitable dog with a tendency to react too fast goes to a placid man who can calm it down. In club we have excitable people with excitable dogs, and slow moving people with stolid dogs; and it's almost impossible to get results unless the owner changes himself or herself entirely; you can't change the dog!

If I had known about the long DOWN when Chita was young my life would have been different as she would have learned easily while tiny, and without much hassle, that I was stronger than she was. As it was, she remained dominant and when grown she knew very well she was stronger than I am. I now use that DOWN when she gets naughty; if necessary I hold her head to the ground, and keep it there, as her mother would have done. That reminds her without any harshness just who is top dog. I am quite literally, on top of her.

Once the dog does lie down quietly, which, with ten dogs this time is in the third week but with the other two will not happend for some weeks yet, we can progress. Our two boss dogs have to learn; and the only way they will is for the owners to keep them down for the whole lesson with all their force. Once the dog realises it is no use battling, and submits, going down fast by himself on the command, we can go on. Brute force any way other than this just doesn't have results, as far as I can see, with a very dominant dog, unless the owner is a very large strong man. Women have to be more subtle, especially with big dogs.

Most small dogs learn fast that you are stronger than they are; you can pick them up! If a little dog defies me up he comes, up in the air in front of my nose and is held there at arm's length (not cuddles as that is consoling and rewards him for bad behaviour). He needs punishing; this is often a dog that has tried to bite and must be told off, or he can't be cured.

Club, once we have managed to begin proper training, is very far from being a solemn affair. It is often great fun, as dogs are natural clowns.

One dog I miss is Smithy. Smithy is a Golden Retriever, a big solid fellow, with much better body and bone than Janus, and a darker coat. Janus is apricot-coloured and has never developed a silky coat. Smithy is a much richer colour with a lovely coat.

Smithy had a habit of falling in love each club night. He invariably fell in love with a different animal; usually it was a bitch, but one night he took a fancy to a very masculine little Sheltie about a quarter his size that has been used as a stud dog.

It was very difficult to do any work that night, as Smithy yearned and if possible pulled his owner over towards the Sheltie. The Sheltie stalked away, every inch of him showing that he was offended at this extraordinary behaviour. Being a very fluffy little dog, and of the same breed as two bitches we have, probably Smithy never did get close enough to find out he was wrong. He sat and languished, reducing us all to laughter.

He was far from easy to train, and his owner is slightly built. Smithy co-operated after a fashion. He has a lovely temperament so that is never a problem, but he was difficult to teach.

One night we were sending the dogs through the tunnel. This is a Mr Man tunnel we got from a mail order catalogue. It is made of plastic, about eight feet long and covered in little painted Mr Men. Most dogs, once they have mastered it, love it. Chita goes through it over and over again if I let her. She rushes in, bounces out, and runs round to do it again, full of excitement. This is fun!

Smithy, the first time he met the tunnel, seemed to think there might be a demon hidden inside. He refused even to try. His owner knelt at the end with pieces of liver, putting her hand halfway down to try and entice him through, but still Smithy refused. Finally I suggested she put him on the lead, crawled through herself, and coaxed Smithy to follow.

Smithy's expression as he watched his owner get down on hands and knees and vanish was a delight. He couldn't believe his eyes. A moment later he rushed through and bounced at her in excitement, knocking her sprawling. He soon enjoyed the tunnel too.

Smithy is retired now, and Angela and Geoff, his owners, have a young dog, Kelly. Kelly is also a character. Though the same breed as Smithy, he is even paler than Janus, a dark creamy gold, and he is quite different in character to their older dog. Geoff trains him. Kelly does also need a lot of waking up to work, but in a different way to Smithy.

It is never possible to work out exactly what one

will do on a training night. There is a rough guideline, but it has to be adapted, as some dogs may fail to understand one particular exercise, which means the owner hasn't understood it, and you have to rethink the way it is being taught. Others are slower at quite a different exercise. Or someone says something that makes you realise you have not made yourself absolutely clear; they mistook what you said and have been teaching the dog wrongly. That is very easy to do.

I try to go back to my problems with my dogs, when I was first learning to train. You may know a great deal about dogs and the way they behave, but the way you teach them in order to train them has to be learned.

So many people fail to realise dogs don't understand our language. Until they know what SIT means, you have to show them, using the lead as a guide, your hands on their bodies as a guide, your voice saying the word in the right tone, and then you must say 'good dog' in a nice tone, or the dog fails to understand it has pleased you. Tone is far more important than what you say. Timing of the commands and timing of praise are important too.

Each dog needs different timing. Janus is relatively easy in that he is a ponderous dog, and I can now anticipate most of his actions if I watch him, and stop him doing something undesirable. Puma never reacted without a command, as she watched me intently. Like all dogs that have been kept in kennels for some time, she had to learn to adapt to the big wide world, and also had to learn to play and respond to me. This takes about two years with most dogs. We have had several in club who had been sold at two years old by a breeder who had to cut back on stock. Chita watches me intently but she is dominant, and also eye-sensitive, and so fast that I have had to speed myself up, and even then she sometimes reacts faster than I do, and that is when she will give chase.

Every dog you live with gives you a new dimension, and I had a major advantage just before I started the dog club. A neighbour of ours, who has now become a friend, asked if I could do her a favour and train her twelve-week-old Yellow Labrador pup, Boy.

Miss Marchel is French, though she has lived over here since the second World War. She owns a farm, and at this time, now almost eight years ago, she was waiting for an operation for a replacement hip. If there is one thing you can't do on crutches, it is train a pup.

I started training Boy some months before I bought Chita. He was tremendous fun. He is quick, alert, and eager to learn, but he is also not too fast a dog, so that the two of us clicked. I went down to the farm every afternoon, walked my dogs, did a bit of training with them, and then devoted an hour to Boy.

Boy made me realise how easy life is for some people. He is from working stock, and learned so easily that everything I did with him felt like cheating; it took very little hard work.

Miss Marchel was delighted with Boy's progress. I went on with him for about a year, even after I bought Chita. He was relaxation after her, too, as Puma was. Boy's owner wanted to pay me but how on earth do you charge for having so much fun? I asked if I could use her fields for my dogs; to train Chita to track; to let them romp free, safely away from stray dogs and roads.

I now have the freedom of the farm, which is lovely. There are eighty acres of fields, and though much of the year they are under crops, for weeks at a time I have stubble to track on. A couple are under grass, which we can use when the cattle are off them.

You never know where an apparently insignificant action will lead. The use of those fields has helped to control Chita as tracking tires her far more than walking does. I knew, after training Boy, that I would have no trouble at all with a new tiny pup.

The gods were laughing!

I had a new lesson to learn, but in those halcyon days with my little spare-time biddable dog, I was quite unaware of what lay in store with Chita. Maybe it is as well that none of us can read the future.

CHAPTER FIVE

When I started the dog club I knew quite a bit about dogs but nothing at all about running a club. Those who joined the club had, mostly, never been to a club before. This is a big advantage as the worst possible newcomer for my club is someone who has moved here from a big city club. They have no idea what life is like in a rural area, and they are often full of advice on changing all the rules, making all the owners work far harder, having more instructors (apparently conjured out of thin air) and whatever they do decide invariably means ten times as much work as I can handle – as, of course, they have no intention whatever of doing any themselves.

They can also cause problems by constant criticism, both to me and behind my back, as they compare the little club to its total detriment with a club with ten times the membership, with a very supportive, active and flourishing committee and the ability to put on shows; and at least ten instructors if not more.

The result is that their strictures are taken as gospel and since show people travel countrywide, a club can gain a totally undeserved reputation because one member did not find within it what he or she wanted, which in some cases is the ability to go on with competition training, which I can't give as I don't run classes for just one owner and one dog. I have around thirty owners and thirty dogs to consider at any one time. All most of mine want is to get on terms with a domestic pet.

Few people ever stop to remember that those of us who run my kind of club are unpaid. We give up our time for nothing.

I hoped when I started I would have plenty of help by now. I keep on hoping! No one can help with the teaching as no one knows enough about training their own dogs yet. You can't teach others to do something you have not done yourself. I have not won in competition; I have however had full marks in every single part of the Trials requirements at one time or another, except the track for which we got as our highest mark 91/95. That we don't get full marks every time is simply because none of us is always perfect; dogs vary in their responses, or there is a variation in an exercise we have never met. I can teach every exercise that we do well ourselves.

Chita nearly always has full marks for her agility and full marks for her search. Full marks on that exercise is rare.

So people can criticise to their heart's content (people being people they will!) but I know my capabilities; and I know those of my bitch. I have no unrealistic visions of reaching the top with her; she is nervous, becomes agitated and needs my reassurance and will get it, never mind if it loses me marks. I take the same attitude with my dog club. I have no intention of aiming at heights I know none of my owners will ever reach or, most of them, want to reach.

It has taken seven years to work out how best to run the club. The committee now is a social committee only and has nothing whatever to do with training. That is my province; how I run it, how I run the tests and how I run the classes are my decisions alone.

This is far better as before I was like the man with the donkey. He started out with his son riding. People said, 'Poor old man. Look at that boy riding while his father walks.' So the boy got off the donkey, and his father got on. People said, 'Look at that wicked old man riding that poor little donkey, while his son walks. 'So they both got on the donkey. People said, 'Look at those wicked people both riding on that poor little donkey.' So they got off the donkey and carried it!

My first committee was marvellous, but their dogs learned to behave and they left. Committees change every year and I only have one vote so that one committee might decree we only took in RSPCA rescue dogs; another might insist all awkward dogs left and we only took in very easy dogs (they don't need help!) and yet another had the bright idea of getting all dogs including puppies up to full competition standard in twelve weeks, never mind if it was old Mrs Jones who was nearly eighty with her tiny Yorkie, or the little lass with a Labrador that would have sorted out her father, never mind her.

I no longer have children training dogs; it is far too difficult for them. A child of ten has not enough physical co-ordination herself (or himself), does not concentrate and is not patient enough for what is a very demanding job. No man who shoots, or a shepherd, or police dog handler, allows his family to mess about with his dog in training. The training is regarded as a very highly skilled and very carefully thought-out part of the pup's life. Someone giving a wrong command, or failing to enforce a given command could cost the shooting man his dog, if for instance it failed to obey him when told to sit still and ran in front of the guns. A police dog playing the fool and failing to obey might even cost the policeman his life. It is a very skilled type of training.

Few people realise it is a skill. I wish men owners of the guarding breeds would not send their wives to start the dog; it is fine if they have had a dog before but rarely seems to work if it's their first dog.

Women may be better with pups but are very likely to baby the animal and spoil it. It is then very hard to train. I don't think I would ever have a guarding breed as my first dog; my German Shepherd was my ninth dog, after a variety of terriers, cross breeds and a very stubborn Golden Retriever. Few women are strong enough for a big Rottweiler or a young and boisterous German Shepherd or a Dobermann. I am only just over five feet high and till I learned the knack of checking I found the big breeds almost impossible to handle. Now I can use the sort of voice that makes a dog sit and think and that works wonders.

It is quite funny to watch a dog struggling and refusing to behave, and to say BEHAVE, as every dog on the floor immediately sits up and looks at me in amazement, and for the next few minutes it is bliss!

It is quite difficult to make new owners understand that the only way to control a dog is by teaching it to obey the commands SIT, STAND, DOWN and HEEL fast, instantly and tidily. If the dog is sloppy it is defying the owner (unless of course it is a young and sprawly pup; they can't co-ordinate at first). It is quite ridiculous to keep saying SIT, SIT, SIT, without effect, as it must sit when you say SIT and to repeat the command defeats the whole object of training; you sit now or else; and if it won't sit it is *put* in the sit, fast. Otherwise it is virtually doing a Harvey Smith gesture. 'Oh, OK, I will do it, but my way, so there. You haven't the willpower to make me behave.'

Dogs use all sorts of wiles to get round their owner. It is very difficult to be firm with an adorable bitch puppy lying on her back with her legs in the air; but she *is* defying her owner. So is the dog that wraps its paws round the lead, or its owner's legs. So is the dog that snarls or growls or mouths too forcefully. They all have to be checked, kindly, firmly and once and for all. Be too gentle and all you do is set up a nagging situation that never works as the dog doesn't bother about it. Nag, nag, nag, and the poor dog just blots out this boring noise.

The habit of instant obedience is essential and until the dog does obey it is little short of lunatic to let it run free without a lead. I don't do it even in a confined space until I get instant response to the command COME, as I want my pup to learn to come to me when I call her, every single time; not just now and then. Even with Chita now, at six years old, if she fails to return when called she goes back on the training line and we do nothing for a day or two but play at coming; she runs out and I call her back, giving a little tug if she doesn't come at once, and welcome her wholeheartedly with a game when she arrives. It retrains her fast and without any aggravation on my part, or resentment on hers; it's our fun game for coming. Being domineering when you call the dog is more likely to make it scared of you, and it will return, cowering.

A young dog that won't come back is likely to be run over. We had a club dog run over last session; a young dog running free too near a main road. He saw something on the other side of the road and dashed across and was hit by a car. It is very hard on the driver who has that happen to him. For the dog broken bones will probably mean arthritis early on in life. If he isn't killed. Our dog has a broken pelvis and some internal bruising. He was lucky. Four club dogs have died under cars. At least eight more have been hit by cars or bicycles.

It is very important when training a dog at a club to bring it every week without fail, as the training should be a slow continuous progression. The fact that it isn't in many clubs is because owners come in when they please, as if it didn't matter whether they were on time or not. Then they may not come for two or three weeks, and no progress is possible. All that usually happens is heartbreak for the instructor who is fighting a losing battle against owners' apathy and who then gives up, and either struggles on not caring much, or closes the club.

I have become quite ruthless. People who are persistently late are either asked to leave or come into the last class which is not aimed at doing much more for the newcomers than socialise the dog and teach them a little ready for the next full session, as these people have joined in the middle of a course. A persistently naughty dog that does not progress and creates trouble, and does not come regularly, which means no progress is possible, is asked to leave.

As far as I am concerned I get little out of the club except exhaustion and a lot of hard work for nothing whatever in return, *except* that when I see the progress most dogs make it is worth every moment of my time.

Recently Jane came back to visit us. Jane and Heidi, her yellow Labrador, were memorable as they came to club for the first time about three years ago, at about ninety miles an hour, and hit the far side of the room. Jane, looking as if about to burst into tears, stood there, bright red, and glared at me. As far as she was concerned she hated her dog yet loved her and didn't want to give up on her.

Heidi was almost as difficult as Chita. Jane and I sweated blood over her; we despaired over her, we fought to make her see sense which was something she never wanted to see as her idea of life was to hurtle through it at top speed, all the time. 'CHECK Heidi. SIT Heidi. Jane, make her behave. Jane, you have to be tougher.'

Jane isn't tough; she is charming and to have a dog that needed a stroppy man on the end of the lead was at first a nightmare for her. Jane soon realised, as I had with Chita, that either she did become tougher, or Heidi went; probably for that much-dreaded one-way trip to the vet. Heidi, untrained, would be as much trouble as Chita and impossible to live with easily. A dog that is a constant headache is a misery in the home.

I had Heidi's double sent to me last year by one of the vets as it was quite impossible. He was stronger than Heidi, was also a Labrador, and he had two ideas in his head. One was to leap at your face and flatten you (with misplaced love admittedly) and the other to lunge on the lead and dislocate your shoulder. I nearly crippled myself showing his owner how to cope. I decided to show the lowest class how their dogs would behave if they failed to train as I taught them. That night was memorable as everyone was appalled at the way the dog behaved and the strength needed to correct it. By the end of half an hour it was walking to heel with me and it continued to do so while I took it. But his owner had to learn how to check him and she did not have the knack and found it impossible to learn it.

She came for four weeks and then decided this was no way to spend her life and the dog went back to its breeder. Since the breeder had said don't train it till it's a year old she or he only got what they deserved. It was then fourteen months old. The dog was probably sold at once to some other unfortunate, if it hasn't been put to sleep.

Jane, however, persisted.

By the end of their first year I was bringing Jane and Heidi out to show new owners how a dog should behave. I asked Jane to go and talk to unhappy people with dogs that seemed not to understand anything and tell them how she and I had battled with Heidi.

Jane's husband, Angus, was transferred, to my sorrow, and Jane left. She has written to me occasionally ever since, and has even introduced me, by letter, to someone who has read my books and hopes one day to meet me at York Trials. I had to cancel this year because of a torn tendon in my knee and Pam's letter cheered me a little, as it starts: 'Dear Joyce, Damn, damn, damn. When are we going to meet?' Which echoed my sentiments as I was not only intending to go to Trials but meeting Jane and Angus, meeting Pam and going over to see my grandchildren on the day after the Trials.

Jane and Angus were here two weeks ago on holiday and came to visit us. Nobody at the club except Sally Clark, our chairman, remembered Jane as most have come since she left. They watched this lovely partnership, dog and owner working together, enjoying every second, while Heidi's tail never stopping wagging; Heidi lay at the side of the hall, behaving perfectly no matter what went on, and I went home that night feeling nine miles high, knowing that for Jane I had worked a tiny miracle and helped her to get on to terms with what is now the most beautiful bitch anyone could own.

She might not win any prizes for beauty; I haven't looked at her that way. I never am much impressed by first prizes in the Breed ring as it's so much a matter of opinion. One judge would like Puma and award us a First Prize and, the next week, out we go with what judges in Beauty kindly term 'the rubbish'.

What I want in a dog is brains and kindness and the ability to be a companion and have fun with his owner, never mind whether or not it has a pedigree. Toby, our funny little Staffordshire Bull Terrier-cross, who was a wicked little dog, has a very secure place in my heart, though no judge of Breed would ever look at him twice.

Heidi still needs work and Jane has never let up, though she no longer goes to a dog club. It is people like Jane who keep us all going; the rare success among so many that fell by the wayside and disappointed us. It was too much trouble; they didn't have ten minutes a day to spend on the dog; they couldn't be bothered to come that night; it was raining. I turned out one night for four people only in vile weather. I no longer run club if there is ice or snow. It is automatically cancelled.

They have jobs so no time for training. I have a job. They have a house to run. So have I. They have husbands. So have I. I do our shopping and cooking, and have two dogs and a cat and a family who may visit and be told, 'Sorry, I'll be back about ten-thirty; it's dog club. Get your own supper, will you?'

I often wonder why on earth some people buy dogs.

CHAPTER SIX

During the seven years that I have been running the club I have found it necessary, almost every session, to sit down and think very hard. The sixth to seventh week of any class, whether it is dogs, music, driving, weightwatching, is fall out and complaints week. I call it the Grouse Season.

Julie, who came to me for help with her two Shelties, Mischief and Princess, was my weight-watching instructor some years ago. We began to compare notes; and if dog club and a new weightwatcher class started at about the same time, we got the fallers-by-the-wayside and the grumbles in the same week. It seems to be a fact of life.

I collect the complaints and think about them. Some are valid; and if so I try to do something about them. Some are beyond my remedy, as I run a *pet* club; I do not do competition work. I do not base my teaching on competition work, though a clever handler can easily adapt it, so those who want competition invariably blame me. They want club changed for their benefit, forgetting that a club consists of all its members; not just the small minority.

Last session but one we had no progress whatever; I was badly bitten by a dog whose owner failed to tell me he had nasty habits. I had four stitches in my hand and was out of action for two weeks (luckily for the club in their Easter break). As a result I decided I had to be very firm from now on, both with new-comers, as to the type of dog they bring me and with those who regard dog club as somewhere to come if they have nothing better to do.

Their dogs show no sign of progress and are a confounded nuisance to say the least, as they disrupt the class and mean we have to go back to the beginning for the sake of someone who can't be bothered to give up even one half an hour a week regularly for their dog.

My colleague Sally Clark hadn't been well, but had struggled on, probably adding to her troubles as both of us were getting overwrought about the club problems. Club secretaries are invariably among the six-week-leavers and so are our treasurers, so that I always end up like Bill the Lizard in *Alice in Wonderland*. Joyce will do it. Joyce does do it; books the hall and banks the money; books the judges and sorts the classes; copes with squabbles and personality conflicts which occasionally seem to arise for no good reason; Joyce prepares the books for audit, keeps the accounts, buys the trophies, and smiles perhaps not too sweetly when, after struggling to complete writing a book, done the family shopping, answered the phone to those whose dogs are ill, then has to listen while everyone else explains they haven't done their homework as they were busy!

The end of the evening, after taking four classes of about ten people each, coping perhaps with an unusually awkward dog and several unhappy owners whose dogs aren't progressing, may well end up with a verbal attack on me (of course with the *best* of intentions) for being a lousy teacher, needing to do this, that and the other to improve the club, and while wishing on me a great deal more work and organisation, all of it unpaid, doing nothing whatever but snipe, and not help!

I do love people like that!

The other morale-boosting statement is 'If I went to so-and-so every week my dog would be marvellous,' the inference being my dog isn't marvellous because I have only got rotten old you! The fact that no dog is trained in ten minutes seems to escape the person concerned or maybe they don't know that!

Fortunately the vast majority of the club want only to get their dogs civilised for taking around and don't make demands beyond my capacity.

This year has been interesting as the club has grown and having decided to ignore everyone's advice and work out my own way of running it since I am the only instructor and no one else knows enough to help, it has been far easier to run. Our dropout rate this session is confined to one handler out of thirty, which is far below our usual rate of about twelve out of that number. Last session only five left. One of those moved away; another has a demanding job and had done what he wanted with his dog. Another had only come to cure the dog of barking too much and that being done there was no further need to train the dog as she was already very well behaved. Two grumblers departed.

One of the main grouses in any club is the record book of attendance and payment. It is necessary to keep a check on what comes in and to make ends meet. Our hall costs about £112 for three months and then there is insurance; and we have trophies, photostatted homework sheets, and sell books on dog training when new members come. We are registered with the Kennel Club which means we must be audited so foolproof books have to be kept. I find this a headache as I can't do arithmetic!

Club members pay 80p a night; they would bring five- and ten-pound notes so we needed a float which always got mixed in with the club money and had to be removed; someone would pay two weeks or three weeks in arrears and we couldn't just say twenty came and twenty paid as twenty came and two didn't pay and one paid for a month; the end of club night found Sally and me sitting at the table, fending off questions like 'can I have a new lead', as that would mean we had to start balancing again; with blinding headaches, and five pence too little or a pound too much.

I would forget about the float and bank it and then nothing balanced!

We once spent three utterly miserable days over the audit, and at that point I sat down and thought hard and reorganised everything. People think I am inconsistent and change my mind; in fact I have tried out something, often suggested by somebody else, found it impossible to manage and tried to improve and make life easier for Sally and myself, as most of the work falls on the two of us. The lion's share falls on me as I do all the teaching now.

I discovered that Findon Club, where my friends Pat O'Shea is one of the instructors and Anne Malcolm Bentzen is secretary, pay in advance. Since they have been running their club for about twelve years or more, compared with my seven, they are among my main advisers. The other is one of our vice-presidents, who is on a number of high-up committees and can help me operate the Kennel Club rules. If we do have a club problem, he points out it is due to someone who is actually in breach of a club rule that I can use to sort it out without too much hassle. The Kennel Club regulations can be a godsend in club because they are designed to cover varying types of complaints.

For instance our aims, as defined in our rules and approved by the Kennel Club, are to run a *pet* club only; if we want to change the nature of the club we have to hold an emergency meeting or change it at the Annual General Meeting and then only with the approval of threequarters of the members. It has been tried, but since more than threequarters are happy to keep it as a pet club, it has never been changed. If it were, I would leave as I don't propose to train very advanced and complicated techniques for nothing.

Those who do have my greatest respect as it is very demanding; you have to think so hard about every individual dog as no two dogs react alike, train alike, or respond alike.

Paying by the session has made life very much simpler, as most of the takings are banked the first week; the club is paid for in advance for three months as there is enough money to cover that and only two entries need to be made. Dribs and drabs of money come in, but they can be left and entered on the first of the month, instead of a weekly effort to make it balance; so far there has been no problem at all as if one of the few that pay by the week, owing to having shift work to contend with, does pay for the month then it's held over and entered once a month, not by a sort of 'not this week, but next week' code to myself.

My bank manager very kindly audits us for nothing, and I don't use petty cash. Everything is paid by cheque and receipted, so that the bank statements become the audit with only explanatory notes needed in the audit book of each cheque and why it was paid out and so on.

It is fine when everything goes smoothly but, oh dear, when people complain, and blame me for their dogs' bad behaviour when they haven't done the work; and the books won't balance; and the audit is due; and it's nearly Christmas, with all the resulting shopping and cooking and planning and cards and presents to buy and write and send; and the weather is bad and Chita needs training and my deadline is approaching and it rains or snows or freezes, life gets hard! I meet Sally in the woods, where anyone would think we had an assignation, as we both walk dogs there and often meet by accident, even when trying to avoid one another as we have seen each other's cars and don't want to stop and chat, which we do! 'It's no use,' I say, 'I'm fed up,' I say, 'I hate it,' I say. 'Everyone is complaining about me and everyone is having bright ideas to improve the club which no one but me is ever going to act on as they are prepared to beef and suggest but never ever do any work. I am giving up. I am jumping in the Straits; I am going to Bermuda; I am getting *out*.'

'It's a crazy way to spend my time when nobody ever is pleased, or says they are pleased, or behaves as if I have helped.'

These cries from the heart may come standing on a wet path on top of the cliffs in the rain, with me dashing through a Janus walk, as if Chita isn't trained I am going to suffer; she is still as fast as ever and can be as naughty as ever if she thinks I am not going to be as fierce with her as I need to be. She is lying down; just; under control; just; and Janus is probably sitting in a floppy lollop with a particularly silly expression on his face as if he thought humans were pretty daft anyway, and Susie and Kim, Sally's dogs, are lying beside her. Susie is a Boxer and Kim is an Old English Sheepdog and both are as awkward as they come, though nowhere near as bad as Chita. The dogs are quite obviously all longing for these two idiots to get their natter over and carry on walking, and we finally roar with laughter and rush off in different directions, having decided that life is one big laugh and what do my silly woes matter anyway?

Tuesday comes round again (they do come fast!) and I manage somehow to get through my work and train Chita and have some kind of scratch meal which leaves me guilty as it's far from my diet, and drive off and land in club, ever-hopeful.

They come in; the dogs bright-eyed and prick-eared and happy, tails wagging, pulling to me, and I have to ignore them, as if I fuss them their owners will find they keep trying to come to me; I watch the adorable German Shepherd puppy bounce in her corner, and see dogs that last week weren't lying down all lying down as their owners wait for me to mark them off in the register, as we wait for all to come and the class to begin.

Ten quiet dogs. I think back to that first night and agitated owners with dogs pulling in all directions; owners not sure what we were going to ask of them; owners who knew their dogs were awful and would never train; owners who had bought a puppy with the best of intentions and found they had bought a headache. By the ninth week I have achieved heaven, with all the dogs under control, with handlers who will relax and smile and crack a joke, come in with a dog walking quietly at their side and with beaming faces.

It is never easy to make people understand that the way they move can affect their dogs. A lively person may trigger the dog to near-lunacy; she or he moves fast and the dog moves fast. Whatever I do with Chita has to be done slowly or she overexcites and becomes unmanageable. Race to the door or the phone and the dog races too; everyone yells at everyone else and the dog joins in too; why be quiet when the whole family makes a din? Barking is often the only way he can get any attention.

One dog in particular I remember vividly from five years ago as she had a tendency to bite and had already bitten at least one person. She was far from well controlled. The owner complained so bitterly, railing at me for lack of progress, that I broke my usual rule of trying to be polite (it's very hard to keep at times!) and said: 'It's entirely your own fault. The dog is *your* boss.' She was so furious with me she walked out there and then.

I didn't expect to see her again but the next week I was talking to the caretaker when I heard a yell of SIT. Then, HEEL. I watched as that owner and her dog walked perfectly down the corridor.

'Great!' I said. 'What happened to you?'

'I could have killed you!' she said. 'But you were right.'

That became one of the best dogs in club and when she left because she had full control and did not want to work for Obedience or Trials competition I had a letter saying: 'Thank you. But for you my dog would have had one bite too many.'

I so rarely get letters to thank me that I kept it to remind me, when I feel dog club is punishing me too much, that it does have major rewards as if that dog had bitten again she would now be dead. Training teaches control, changes the nature of the dog from dominant to submissive, provided the owner keeps it up, and a biter won't do it again as the dog knows it won't get away with it and will suffer for its sins. That dog is alive and very happy and they are all delighted with her.

It is difficult for those who compete in Breed and only value prizes, or those who compete in Trials and Obedience and only value prizes, to understand how anyone gets satisfaction from the dog as a dog; I don't remember which poet wrote or why (and don't tell me I have quoted wrong as I don't know where to look it up!): 'Mongrel, puppy, whelp and hound and cur of low degree.' They all matter as far as I am concerned.

I am not in the least interested in kudos for running a club; offhand I find it a silly way at times to spend my life! Someone on a course once told me with great pride that she was secretary of a dog club and *he* was her chairman. I felt an awful desire to say 'Big Deal' and curtsey as obviously I was supposed to be terribly impressed. I don't get impressed; someone who reads the news on TV to me is just a newsreader, not some sort of demigod. Some people are famous for quite the wrong reasons. They don't have many virtues as people; the people who do are like most of those who come to club; they do their best, they try their hardest and live quietly and unobtrusively and discreetly and never make the headlines.

They don't give me many problems either; they have come for a specific reason, to learn to train a dog that is out-of-hand; they do so and leave. I enjoy them and their dogs, especially when, having learned by their first mistakes, and had my help in retraining the dog, they come back with their second dog as a puppy; that really is a pleasure.

CHAPTER SEVEN

It is extremely hard to write about a specialised field and make it entirely understandable to someone who lives in an urban environment and knows nothing about animals, or to explain how one teaches in a dog club to those who know nothing about dogs.

Every club is run differently. Some have everyone come at the same time, spend the whole evening there, provide tea and coffee, and run it as a social club. Some are only to train dogs for competitive work and those are run on much more military lines, with dogs and people working in parade-ground style, as the police do. These are usually run by people who compete at very high levels.

Those able to benefit from a club like this are extremely fortunate, as it isn't possible for someone like myself to groom a Crufts winner; I have never been taught by anyone who has had Crufts experience, except very briefly on one-week courses about once a year.

There are, however, all over the country, many people like myself, who, though not training dogs primarily to win Crufts Obedience, have lived with them, worked with them and been with several dogs daily for many years. We know how they behave when running free, how they respond when we command them for normal daily obedience, and have, during our lives, owned a number of dogs which we kept until they died of old age. Since we are experienced in living with dogs, we do have a great deal more knowledge than the owner who has just bought a puppy for the first time.

The type of club I run is much more relaxed; I have a class every hour, from six pm until 10 pm. The dogs that have just joined come at six; those that have been there for more than twelve weeks at seven; puppies and those who join after a course has begun start at eight; and those who want more advanced work at nine. It is very demanding and quite exhausting.

We progress not at a set rate, but at the rate that each dog demands. Some dogs learn fast and others learn slowly. One class may consist almost entirely of dogs that are incapable of progressing at speed; another of dogs that can go further than most. No two groups are ever alike or learn at the same speed.

Once the session has begun I may change people and their dogs around; a nervous dog will be better in the puppy class, where everything is much smaller than he or she is; a fast-learning mature pup might do better brought into the class for beginner dogs, and made to go at a faster speed. It is quite impossible to be didactic. You simply play it by ear, as each session brings different problems, different responses from the dogs and different progress.

Dog Training Weekly, which publishes the Working Trial and Obedience show results, also carries correspondence pages. Here competitive people may write to say that people like myself, who have never worked a dog at a high level, shouldn't teach at club at all, and as for running a club...well, what can we know?

We can't qualify our own dogs, so how can we possible be competent? Few of these people have had as many years around dogs as those of us who run this type of club; and few of them have had to battle with the types of dog that we have kept and worked and made acceptable in society. They tend to buy a dog, find it difficult, so they sell it and go on doing this until they get a dog that will win.

There is an enormous gulf of misunderstanding between us.

The very competitive club has little time for the pet owner as far too much hard work has to go into the competition dogs or they won't get up to the high standard required. The owner who merely wants to teach a dog manners, to come when called, to sit when told, or lie down when told, or to stand for examination at the vet's, gets very little help, as the teaching is not geared to that type of dog.

The people who come to me want to go out for a pleasant walk with a dog that behaves itself; they want to know how to house train a puppy; whether they are feeding correctly, and giving enough; how to groom their dogs and what equipment to use. They rarely have the right type of lead and chains as what is sold in most pet shops is often shoddy and unsuitable. A badly made lead will break and then your dog is loose, perhaps near a four-lane highway; and that means a dead dog. Good equipment is not cheap but my dogs' leads are over thirteen years old and still as good as new. They are made of the best bridle leather, and I use saddle polish on them. They are stitched, not riveted, and the clips are trigger clips. The scissor clips spring open with a powerful dog and the snap clips straighten out if he pulls suddenly.

I find we need as much theory as practice, or people simply don't understand what they are being taught, why the exercise is done and how to apply it in daily living.

Often we come to a halt as I find people have been practising wrongly at home; perhaps have used an odd signal, and the dog is not performing correctly; he is getting up from a sit position before he is told; or a release command of 'good dog' has somehow become interpreted in the dog's mind as 'OK, I can rush round the room and bark at all the other dogs now!'

There are, of course, many top handlers who are also good dog people, and understand dogs of all breeds. They rarely criticise us. There is a group of people who would like to eliminate the pet owner — who goes to a show to see how his dog is progressing, but is not aimed at top-level Obedience, which is very hard work – from all chance of competition and would prefer to keep it only for those who are on their way to the top. That seems odd, as all of them started as pet owners; few people are born professionals.

I know several people who have won Crufts; every one of them started out at my level, and worked up from it, and long before they got to Crufts, ran clubs for pet owners themselves. People who compete at that level need time, opportunity, a first-class instructor, and to be free of family commitments, as it is essential to travel widely and compete every week, unless you are a very exceptional team.

My work and my family prevented me from living that sort of life until twelve years ago and even now it is not easy to find enough free time for Chita's Trials. I make time for her training as she must have it or she reverts to wildness.

These criticisms can come into club, as of course owners also read *Dog Training Weekly* and become aware of them. Often the critics have had very easy dogs and can't appreciate that all dogs are different. The average pet dog is simply not capable of this type of competitive work. You need a fast-reacting dog that loves learning and has so much energy that it is very difficult to control.

It is no more possible to get every dog born to Crufts standard than to force every child born up to college standard and PhD level.

Often, on courses, the very competitive club trainer will also be very vocal about those of us who, in their eyes, should not be so forward as to try and run a dog club. It is rather nice when our marks come out and we find we have beaten them! I was very lucky in that on both my instructors' courses, which I took during the past six years, Muriel Pearce was my judge.

Muriel owned Obedience Champion Megan of Monksmead, a sheepdog bitch that became a legend. People say 'I was so glad I saw Muriel work Megan before she died', and remember it as a highlight of their lives. I have not seen Muriel work Megan; that was before the days when I had time for training my dogs beyond pet standard, but I have watched her train Letty, her Malinois. She qualified Letty CD ex (Champion Dog excellent) this year. It is impossible to explain to someone who has never seen a really expert handler work a dog just how that differs from most of those who train their dogs, even to Crufts standard.

Those who saw her, say that watching Muriel with Megan was like watching Torvill and Dean, the top world skating pair. There was no one to touch her. Muriel has rhythm of movement, precision of timing and total understanding of the way a dog responds.

Muriel is also a Championship judge and has judged Crufts, which is a very high honour and happens only once in a lifetime. She is at present the Television Commentator for Crufts Obedience, so is well known to all those who watch that every year.

I spent a lot of time, after we had been judged and had our results, talking to Muriel in the bar at the hotel where we stayed. It is always fascinating to talk to an expert. On the second course there was a judging seminar, so that people could learn how to judge at shows, as well as to compete. There were twenty-four on the course and we were all questioned in great detail, as she intended to take only six people and wanted those with most dog knowledge.

I was delighted to be one of the six. I was also delighted with her comment on my paper which was: 'A wealth of knowledge and experience.' As I had come in for a lot of criticism from the competition people, who were in the majority, it was reassuring. The three others who also run pet clubs scored much more highly than most of the competitive people.

So it gave me immense pleasure when Muriel answered a letter I wrote to her by ringing me to ask if she could visit the club one evening. She comes to Llandudno regularly to see her mother.

Ours is a tiny club; most of those who run clubs have help in teaching and I have no one there who knows enough about dogs and their training to do more than back up occasionally as yet. I wondered what she would make of us. I had been reassured by finding, when we met at Trials, that in spite of her past success in Obedience, Muriel was not finding it easy to qualify Letty. She most certainly didn't manage it the first time she tried and, like most of us, had to go to a number of Trials before they gained those coveted points that give you the title. You require 80 per cent to pass, and have to gain 80 per cent in each of the four separate sections. Fail one section and you fail them all, even if you have full marks in the other three sections. It is exceedingly difficult.

Chita can get very high marks in three sections regularly and fail the fourth.

Such silly things can happen at times, which make all the difference between failure and success and have nothing to do with the skill of the dog or the way it has been trained.

On one particular occasion, on a very sunny day, most of the dogs failed their jumps. Letty, Muriel's bitch, also failed, which was very unusual. I was waiting my turn (Letty had jumped before Chita) and as I watched the next dog go over, I realised that the jumps were so set that every dog was taking off into the sun.

We had one of those absurd pieces of luck that can make all the difference. Just before Chita began the six-foot scale a cloud came over; she did all her work without that bright glare in her eyes that had caused some of the other dogs to come to the top of the scale, find themselves blinded and fall back again. She was one of the few that had full marks for that section.

There is so much more to contend with than many people realise. When those jumps were set up the sun would have been in quite a different position in the sky so that the dogs that jumped before lunch did not have the same hazard.

There was a good deal of moaning, not surprisingly, as it was very bad luck for those dogs that were blinded by the sun.

Muriel laughed about it; she never blames her dog. We met several times after that at other Trials. Both Chita and Letty failed the search on one occasion, as did many other dogs. That was a very windy day and it may have been difficult for them to pick up the scent from the articles which had been rammed into the ground to keep them anchored. This may well have caused the smell of disturbed earth to overlay the human smell that the dogs had been taught to find.

It is impossible to be sure, as none of us really knows how a dog smells, what it smells, or how a track or search area feels to the dog itself. We can only guess. It makes for so many differences of opinion and so many arguments, which add to the scene, so long as people don't get too dogmatic about a theory, as it can only be a theory. There is no way of proving it with an animal that can't talk and put us wise.

Dog training is full of controversy. Some people are very didactic and apply rigid rules to all dogs as if all dogs were alike. I find this absurd. One of the top trainers of all, Charlie Wyant, another of the

Crufts all-time Greats, says at the end of his book on dog training (*Heelaway Your Dog*): 'If your method works, don't use mine. You will only confuse the dog.'

Muriel watched the club dogs and, in particular, our very dozy English Setter. It is fairly easy, once you have had some experience, to calm down a lively dog. The dog that is really difficult to teach is the dog that just will not liven up at all. It walks round in a daze, unresponsive, unhappy and defeating the owner who becomes demoralised. Everyone else gets results from their dog and this dog won't perform at all.

In that event you try everything to see what will work: running, larking about, using a squeaky toy, a ball, a feather, rustling crinkly paper, rattling coins in pocket, and as a last resort a piece of liver, as it's far better to get the dog to want to respond than to leave it in its totally depressed state.

I didn't introduce Muriel to the lower classes as it was unlikely that any of them watch Crufts. They were new owners just starting. Occasionally, however, someone has read a book on training, and usually picks the wrong book for my type of club. The books I recommend are Charlie Wyant's *Teaching Your Dog* and *Heelaway Your Dog*, John Holme's *The Family Dog* and for the sheepdog owner, also by him, *The Farmer's Dog*, which are quite the best books around on those subjects, and John Cree's *Training the Alsatian* which is being republished as *Training the German Shepherd*, as the name has been changed in the last few years to what it was before the Great War, when all things German were taboo. Many books are out-of-date; others are for very advanced people. Another good simple one is *Good Dog* written by Jack Howell who trained police dogs.

Some of the older books and some instructors say you should never use titbits, as you can't in competition, and it is not a good idea. Professionals, such as the police, shepherds and gundog men, never use them. But they can be very useful for puppies when learning, for nervous dogs, rescued dogs, and for elderly ladies to use as they do not have the physical strength to manage the dog in any other way. Their use must be taught correctly, though, as there are wrong ways of using titbits too.

John Cree uses them. So does Charlie Wyant, and so does Roy Hunter, who used to train police dogs and now runs a training club in Essex. All three men have competed at top level for many years. They don't, of course, use titbits when competing, only at the start of training young dogs. John owned and trained Scottish Working Trials Champion Quest of Ardfern; and Charlie has made up a number of Obedience champions. Roy has trained his own personal dogs as well as his police dogs up to the top stake in Working Trials, so I am by no means out on a limb.

I had at this time one member, now left, who insisted to all and sundry that you never use titbits and I was quite wrong in advocating them. As it was making life difficult I had temporarily stopped them in class, to avoid arguments while I was teaching and not from my own conviction. I had been waiting for an opportunity to reintroduce them in such a way that those who were wavering and whose dogs would benefit would see the point of their use.

Muriel gave me the opportunity.

One of our owners is Angie. (We only have six surnames in club among forty members, as most are Jones or Williams or Hughes or Pritchard, so we use Christian names. We have eighteen people with the surname Jones.) Angie has an English Setter. Petra is particularly reluctant to work; she seems half-asleep all the time and Angie has done very well to get anything out of her at all. As Angie is keen, it is rather sad. She would do very well with some of our very likely dogs. She has to work five times as hard as the owners of those to get any response from Petra.

Out Angie went on to the floor, Petra doing her usual half-alive amble beside her. Angie tried livening her up, tried running, tried using her hands under the bitch's chin. Petra walked on, head down, not in the least interested in anything Angie did or said.

Muriel, watching, said: 'Oh, Joyce, do get that dog switched on. Haven't you any liver?' I had as that afternoon I had been training Chita to perform a new exercise she finds very confusing. She gets upset but if rewarded when it is done right, she soon learns, instead of remaining puzzled and upset. 'Oh, I get a titbit when I do that; so that's what she wants!'

The liver is baked hard and cut into pieces about an eighth of an inch square; just a taste. Muriel always has them when with dogs.

I gave Angie a few pieces. Petra, at the scent of liver, perked up and began to perform beautifully, much to everyone's relief as it is sad to see a dog that doesn't want to try. It seems silly to persist on rigid lines when something so simple has such a remarkable effect. The dog learns through the titbit to enjoy training for its own sake, and also as fun and rewarding. You always praise verbally as you give the titbit reward and the dog learns then that praise is also a reward, and once it has learned that it will respond without giving it food.

People who use a toy to gee the dog up and then throw it as a reward in fact are also using a titbit; it isn't food but has exactly the same effect.

I had to avoid Muriel's eyes a few minutes later as she was told you never do use titbits as you mustn't in the ring. I heard the non-titbit-user saying to someone else that Muriel will never win with her dogs!

In fact that owner has a very lively dog that works happily without any titbit at all, with a toy to attract him. Circumstances do alter cases. I never needed titbits for Puma; Janus works happily for a toy; Chita needs a variety of methods to help her learn as she is extremely nervous and nerves can inhibit learning altogether.

I did introduce Muriel to the top class. We spent the rest of the evening in laughter as she began to reminisce about her experiences when she had Megan.

The laughter escalated when I asked Sally to show Muriel our anti-sheepchasing exercise and how we begin to teach it. The handler runs down the room and drops the dog in the down position. The dog must drop instantly, on command. Ultimately a handler can drop a dog running off at top speed in an instant and prevent a chase.

Sally had hurt her foot and was wearing flipflops, which are not a good idea on our tiled floor. Unfortunately there was no way she could put a shoe on her bandaged toe. Susie is good at this exercise. She is a Boxer, mostly extrovert and unflappable, but also is apt to sulk. She has been hard to train as when she first came to club she was chain-shy owing to Sally using the corrective check hard on her. This does not seem to work with Boxers and other thin-furred breeds. It may hurt them more than it does a dog with very thick neck fur.

We are very proud of Susie, as Sally and I have worked together on her, Sally learning all the time, until she gained 98½ per cent in her last test. So Sally was about to show off for both of us.

Down the hall they ran, her feet slid from under her and Sally did the instant drop, and not her dog. Susie stood with such a funny expression on her face that, once we realised Sally was unhurt, we were all helpless with laughter. 'Oh well, if you are going to do it instead of me, then I'll praise *you*. Good girl!'

I hope Muriel won't tell too many people that our version of the instant down is to drop the handler flat on her back!

I asked Muriel if she would give me an opinion on the club. I had a letter from her that I will cherish.

She has said I may quote it.

She wrote:

I very much enjoyed my visit to your club, where it was obvious that you place the well-being and interests of the dog as your first priority.

Unfortunately in these days of high-pressure competition many clubs and instructors lose sight of the fact that dogs are, or should be, companions and members of the family first, and only if they have the ability should they be asked to enter any competition other than the purely domestic one.

Sadly, though, many handlers expect miracles from quite unsuitable dogs and then, if it fails to make the grade, out it goes to another home in order to make room for another unfortunate animal who will only be loved if it reaches the top grade.

These people are not dog lovers, they are only out for self-glorification, and it doesn't matter who suffers so long as they get enough red cards to brag about.

As you know, Joyce, there is so much more in the making of a champion than many people realise. In the first place, you have to get the right *breed* of dog, and then the *right dog* of that breed, which is not as easy as it sounds. (This is for working competitions whether Obedience or Working Trials – J.S.)

The best dog I ever had, workwise, was Megan of Monksmead and she was the only one I did not pick myself from a litter. Knowing at that time nothing about Border Collies, I relied on the shepherd to choose for me.

There must be a moral there as I have chosen all my other dogs and, of course, not one came up to Megan's standard!

Next, you must consider what there is at the other end of the lead because it is no use having a brilliant dog with a wooden handler or the other way about.

Each of the partners must have a natural ability for the job and a natural rapport towards each other.

Certain things can be learned from classes, books and talking to other people, but unless the ability, talent, call it what you will, is there in the first place, no amount of class work or instruction can make you other than an average pair in the ring, but these average pairs are the mainstay of Obedience classes, they enjoy their day out and go home with the occasional First Prize, and perhaps, even get to Crufts, but the really super pairs are very few and far between. I can think of perhaps half a dozen in the last thirty-two years.

However, most people go to classes like yours to train their dogs to behave in society, to teach them to come when called and not to be a nuisance to other people, and I am sure that all the dogs that have gone through your school will thank you for teaching their owners the best way to make a dog's life a happy and useful one.

This is a very reassuring letter to have, as it is not always easy to judge whether in fact other people are right in their criticisms. It is very obvious that luck plays a large part in any career, whether with dogs or anything else. I owe my writing career to a number of pieces of luck. Probably the greatest luck I had was in finding my agents. Without them I would be nowhere as I don't know the markets.

They knew the publishers who would like the kind of books I wrote, and I have been lucky in those as well. But neither my agent nor my publishers could sell me if I didn't sit down and do the work.

Muriel has been lucky in having had Megan, but Megan alone wouldn't have gone anywhere; she had to be trained, and she had to be trained correctly. Muriel is a natural handler, moving beautifully, relaxed and has the greatest asset of all: she *enjoys* her dogs, and other dogs.

I haven't had the right dogs; Janus is a good dog but not top-quality working material; and his deafness gave me a big disadvantage at the time when it mattered most, in his early days of training. Puma had lead poisoning, which makes for retarded brainpower; she had that, poor dog, but with the advice I got from Great Ormond Street on repatterning her by repeated and constant training, using very small degrees of progression in each exercise, I did manage to compete in Obedience with her; not to win, but for fun for both of us.

Chita is hyperactive, nervous and excitable and this winter, after a layoff of a month because I tore a tendon in my knee, we once more have to return to the beginning and I have to retrain her. She is out-of-hand, noisy, refusing to do as she is told (not dangerously but very naughtily), chasing Chia cat, racing, if I don't watch, at Janus and bowling him over, as he is old and easily knocked down and no longer retaliates as he did once by roaring at her, and generally creating mayhem.

I could do as so many people suggest and put my old dog down and my difficult six-year-old down and buy an expensive dog of the right breed from the right breeding, and move house and train it at the right club, and win with it. There are several people who have worked at Crufts who have had eleven dogs since I bought Janus, sold each as no good at the novice stage and bought another, working up to the right dog of the right breeding.

My respect goes to people like Jill Farrell, who is instructor at one of my past clubs, who trained her German Shepherd for seven years and reached Crufts twice with him; he was not from competition breeding; he started as nervous and Jill persisted. She could have got rid of him and bought something much more likely to win, but she trained the pup she bought and brought him up to a sufficient standard to reach Crufts. He was Obedience Dog of 1983. There are others like that. With many it is a matter of luck; with others it's a matter of determinedly going out to buy the right dog and driving it all the way to the top, irrespective of whether the dog can take it or not.

I don't know what other people have as aims in their clubs; many seem only to be interested in bringing everyone up to competition standard, which is unrealistic, but I have tried to sort out what I want in my club. That is mainly to ensure that the owners all understand their dogs and give the dog the best life that is possible for that partnership.

CHAPTER EIGHT

Helene was only fourteen when she first brought Toby to club, more than five years ago. At that time we were able to use the Library Hall, which is a big hall, with a useful amount of space. It is at present on what seems to be permanent loan to the Post Office. Its main drawback was its terrible acoustics; your voice banged off the very high roof (it did not have a ceiling) and if people talked it was quite impossible to be heard except by those standing up to about ten feet away.

We were likely to have anything from ten to thirty people an evening; another hazard of dog club, as at that time we did not divide into groups, but everyone came, everyone stayed and, quite frankly, all most people did was chatter and mess about.

I was running on the lines I had been taught on instructors' courses, and it just did not work. Also at that time, I had shingles, which is a marvellous addition to a voluntary responsibility that is becoming a millstone, and the sheer effort of getting myself there was beginning to tell on me.

Helene, I think, kept me going when I might have given up. I am very glad now that I did not because once I began to use my brains, instead of relying on what other people had taught on courses, I saw what was wrong with most pet clubs, and tried to put it right in mine.

The only course I have found that does deal with the *pet* club, as opposed to that teaching competition work and so dealing with how to lose fewest points in the ring, is Norman Hills Totnes course. Unfortunately when I went on this my father was dying of cancer and I did not benefit fully from it; he had just had an operation that showed him to be incurable and my thoughts were not on the course at all.

When Helene arrived I had no idea why dog clubs always lost so many members; it is taken as a fact of life. Helene is still with me. We have been through a lot together with Toby!

Toby is a Staffordshire Bull Terrier Collie cross. He is a stocky little black dog with a gleaming coat, a curly tail, a swaggering gait and the most gorgeous eyes that sparkle with life.

When Helene brought him first he was recovering from a broken pelvis, due to having been run over, and had on his shoulder what could only have been a knife wound. He had spent most of his days wandering the streets and getting into trouble till Helene took him on. She wanted a dog and hadn't a dog and here was a dog that was certainly unwanted.

I walked over to her. She was a slim girl with long fair hair and a desperate look in her eyes that defied me to criticise her or her dog. Toby was clutched tightly between her legs, emitting one long threatening rumble.

'He'll bite,' Helene said confidently.

That didn't seem the beginning of a beautiful relationship at all. How on earth could a child this age ever hope to get on top of a dog of this nature. It turned out I didn't know Helene or her capabilities. I doubt if other people do either.

The room was full; people were waiting for their class, and here was a dog that could create mayhem in minutes; he did bite everyone, Helene said; and he growled at all other dogs. He was about two years old, an adult dog that had formed very undesirable habits and lived so rough he was an absolute hoodlum.

I put my hand towards his lead and Toby sprang at me. I grabbed the lead and lifted the dog high in the air, in front of my face at arm's length where he swore and raged and fought me. I had no intention whatever of being bitten, or of giving Toby such a timorous lesson that he would revert to his bad habits. He had to learn once and for all and for life that humans were stronger than he was and biting them was not tolerated, ever.

I didn't like doing it, as there were other children in the room and some of them might think this was normal dog training. It is not. It is a once-in-a-lifetime cure for an absolute villain, to save him from the deathchamber.

Slowly the breath went out of him; slowly the fight went out of him; slowly the rage went out of his eyes; he hung there, looking at me. I waited until I saw what I wanted in his expression and then put him down on the floor.

'Don't you ever do that to me again,' I said, making my voice as angry as possible. The rest of the club were staring at me in amazement, probably all ready to report me to the RSPCA, but only a lunatic in charge of a club allows a dog to make contact provided it gives warning; some breeds don't. A raging dog can do maximum harm and cripple someone for life by so damaging their hands that they can't use them again.

Helene was looking at me with an expression in her eyes I couldn't define. I knelt. Toby crawled to me, and climbed on to my lap and leaned against me. He licked my hand. We have been the greatest friends ever since. Toby always greets me with fervour.

'OK,' I said, 'I don't think he'll bite again but if he does *you* will have to do that, or Toby will have to be put to sleep; he isn't safe unless you cure him of biting and fighting.'

Helene learned fast. Any act of defiance on Toby's

part towards her was rewarded with instant action. We never needed to treat him like that again, but he did need correcting on the lead, over and over, till I wondered that Helene persisted.

She came every week. Other children with easy dogs looked smug and I longed to give them Toby and let them find out what life could be like. There was not one single child handler and never has been in club who could have done what Helene has done. Few adults could have done it either. Other children developed a desire to compete and left because I wouldn't teach them; other children had boyfriends and their dogs were forgotten. Helene continued to come.

Somehow she has grown up, almost without me realising it. Toby has developed into a gorgeous little dog, that spends his days with Helene's father who works in the Botanic gardens. The one-time fighter is now called to heel by a whistle as I appear with Chita. In club Helene is by far the best handler in the top group of people who have been coming for some years, and Toby works beautifully for her, his body proud and alert, heeling beside her, well aware that he is behaving well and happy to obey her.

He may still run off if there is a bitch in season near; and he worries people who don't know his breed because he 'talks'. We have several talkers in club; Chita is one of them, though she doesn't talk, she yodels; Sam, also a German Shepherd, whines; Susie and Toby chunter; Susie the Boxer is also a flat-nosed breed and as our other chunterer is Spike the Rottweiler, also a blunt-muzzled dog, rumbling-growling-grunting may well be a characteristic of the flat-nosed breeds. Nobody knowledgeable could possibly mistake it for a growl. Those of us who realise think it funny; a running commentary on us?

'Silly humans, what on earth did they throw that away for if they wanted it, and why hide that thing when a moment ago they were holding it? If they think they can fool my nose they are making a big mistake.'

Toby rewards me more than most other dogs; his biggest problem a couple of years ago was that when he went out for the dumbbell and picked it up he pirouetted in a circle on his hind legs. It was very funny but Helene wanted her club certificate and Toby was going to lose her marks. We did cure him, but I must confess I preferred his own method of doing the dumbbell to our more formal retrieve!

Toby, as his master is part of the Staff at the Botanic gardens, is allowed in the lecture room. To my embarrassment the other day Chita saw him go inside and since dogs went in there, and she was off-lead, she followed, before I realised what she was up to. I called her and she came and I apologised; Helene's father laughed and said: 'She's only a dog.'

Toby came to join us and came to me, tail wagging, and I stroked him and grinned at him.

'Helene's done wonders with him,' I said.

'Oh no. I'm not having that,' said her father, rather to my astonishment.

'What *do* you mean?'

'If it hadn't been for you Helene wouldn't have Toby now,' he said, 'All the credit is yours, not Helene's.'

I couldn't have taught Helene if she hadn't listened and worked hard at home, so it's very much a dual effort, but it's lovely to be appreciated and through Helene I feel inclined to go on, even when some folk are busy telling me what a lousy club it is and the dogs ought to be at a far higher standard and can't we have more interesting sessions with lots more activity?

We can't; as the room is small, the dogs in the early stages of training and unreliable, the handlers inexperienced and I am responsible for their safety. I had one bad bite this year, the only one I have ever had in my life, and I am not risking that sort of thing happening to anyone else.

There is so much to watch when taking a class.

I have to make sure Toby isn't near people who are convinced his chuntering is growling, as if they become nervous it might turn to a growl.

I have to make adults who aren't used to class situations think of class behaviour, as with ten dogs in the room you can't have people rushing around where they choose; it is far too likely to cause an accident. These aren't trained dogs; they are untrained.

Several owners are deaf so they have to be placed where they can hear me and see me if they lipread, and I have to remember to lift my voice all the time. Not easy at the end of three hours when I am tired.

One thing I try to insist on is that everyone is friendly and nobody has delusions of grandeur. At one club that I joined the committee was all-important; they sat by the stage, and the rest of us lowly creatures barely got a civil word, though they always made sure that they took our money. At another, one person always had the same chair. It upset the whole evening if anyone dared take it, even in total innocence as I did on my second night there. 'That's B's chair. Move!' somebody hissed in an agitated whisper. It looked exactly like all the other chairs, but I moved; I couldn't make out ever what was so special about that chair and that position in the room!

It was remarkably silly as the dog 'knew' that was his den, and as soon as his owner, if he was off-lead, tried to call him to come, he rushed off to lie down where he spent most of the evening. I doubt if the owner realised it was her fault and that she should have never been in the same place twice. So I also have to remember to say: 'Where did you stand last week, as you must move or your dog will go back to that place all the time and may fight for it.'

I seem to spend a great deal of time trying to analyse why clubs lose members and what goes wrong.

The real truth seems to me that the aims of some clubs are unrealistic and that the instructors don't understand how to train dogs! They understand how to *compete* with their dogs, may do a lot of winning with them, and they understand too all the gimmicks that mean you may score better marks when in the show ring. They don't understand how you start with a tiny pup or how you teach an owner who has never had a dog before.

They cannot go back and put themselves where they were many years before; and also by allowing scorn to creep into their voices they upset people and put them off. I knew very well that my first instructors thought me an absolute fool. Their voices showed it; they looked at one another with resigned expressions, which supposedly I was too stupid to understand. (I can lip-read and eye-read! — it isn't an advantage; I walked into the room on one course and somebody on the other side of the room said: 'Oh, God, look who's here! That stupid idiot with the mad Golden Retriever.')

Had I had a real expert to teach me then my dog's deafness would have been identified.

So I try to make sure that nobody who comes to my club ever gets such treatment. From me or anybody else. I don't like clubs who say because X has a little dog she shouldn't come. Little dogs need training too, and X may not be able to afford a bigger dog.

One of the greatest characters I ever knew was a Chihuahua who would have made ten of some of the much bigger dogs I have known. Little dogs are still very much all dog!

CHAPTER NINE

You never have a dull moment with dogs. Add thirty dogs to your own responsibilities and life is interesting. Though at times it is very fraught. If there is an emergency in the family and nobody else to take charge, the needs of the dog become a major problem.

Our most memorable occasion was also a major tragedy. Among my first two pupils were Hilary, with her German Shepherd, Max, and Chris, with Max's sister, Shanie. They were Chita's niece and nephew and born when Chita was just a year old, almost to the day, and she was still causing me major problems.

There I was as desperate as any owner can be, with no confidence at all, sure it was me at fault and that I had completely forgotten how to train any dog when along came Chita's niece and nephew. They were both hyperactive, both extremely noisy, yodelling, or screaming, or making shrill yaps more like a Terrier than a German Shepherd, and there were their owners as desperate as I was; and they were only four months old.

If they wanted to lunge, they lunged and pulled their owners with them. Hilary had had three German Shepherds before and had never known anything like Max. It was Chris's first bitch and she didn't know what to make of her. She didn't know dogs were like this.

Most of them aren't. The only thing that afternoon did was to hearten *me*. Hilary had never had a pup like Max before and was as foxed by him as I was by Chita. The three animals were so alike in behaviour it had to be the way they were bred. Max and Shanie had a different mother to Chita, but their father was Chita's brother. Like her, they had more energy than any dog I have ever met since, other than several of her very close relatives.

We worked; we tried to teach them; we battled with them; we struggled with them. Hilary's husband, who is a very big strong man, took the dog for a long walk before he went to work; Hilary walked him, and Hilary trained him, and Max still was ready to go at five in the morning, and completely fresh by bedtime; unlike his owners who were exhausted, as I was, and as Chris now was.

Chris rang me up to ask if Shanie would ever learn. Chris had a much greater problem than Hilary or myself as this was the first dog she had ever owned, let along trained. Quite honestly, if Chita had been my first dog and not one of a succession I don't think I would have kept her. She would have gone to the vet for a one-way trip as it would have been a crime to wish her on anyone else.

We taught them all to come; teaching them to keep to heel was quite another matter as what they saw they wanted and if they wanted it they lunged and had us almost off our feet. Max was a very handsome large strongly built dog by the time he was eight months old. Shanie is very pretty. Neither resembles Chita who is a beautifully proportioned extremely attractive pocket-Venus of a bitch, a little smaller than most but she makes up for it in muscle power.

Chris and Hilary worked, with as much success as I had with Chita. Practically none. Max grew into an enormous dog with even more energy, most of it frustrated energy as nobody but a fully trained police dog handler could have given that dog what he needed. I was becoming aware of this, but did not know whether to tell Hilary. He was bold, whereas Chita and Shanie were both nervous.

Chris and I managed to get over this, but Shanie was not easy to live with and Chris really needed an easy dog. She was full-time nurse to Jerry, who was paralysed from the waist down and spent his life in a wheelchair. Shanie does relax at home; it is visitors that trigger her to excitement, so she was a delight to both of them; and gave Chris a much-needed break when she walked her, but she still behaved badly on the lead, and was also so anxious that if I ever stroked her, she wet herself; which was another of Chita's little ways too.

Chris and Shanie had been coming for ten months when Chris married Jerry. They had a brief honeymoon and Chris came back to club. Our more experienced dogs were working for a display we were to give at the cathedral fête, which was to raise money for the roof repairs. Two nights before the fête, a friend called on me, as Kenneth was away boating, and she was just preparing to go at about eleven pm when the phone rang.

It was Chris, in considerable distress as Jerry had been taken into intensive care and Shanie was howling, being terrified by the sudden eruption of doctor, ambulance men, and ambulance departing with its siren going, and Chris having to leave her. Their neighbours were complaining about the dog's noise, and that had been the last straw. Could I take Shanie?

I couldn't. Puma was blind and Chita pretty impossible and to bring another bitch with my two bitches would be asking for trouble, but at that time we had the owners of a local boarding kennels in club. I told Chris to ring me back in fifteen minutes and as soon as she rang off I rang Carol.

Could she possibly take Shanie? She could and would kennel her free. She would wait up for us to arrive. I had a thirty-mile drive and it was a very wet night, and blowing. My visitor agreed to come with me and when Chris rang I told her to meet me outside the hospital, with Shanie, in half-an-hour.

I hastily leashed each of my dogs and took them outside and then put them to bed; locked up; and about eleven-fifteen pm we departed, through the dark. By the time we met Chris she knew Jerry was not expected to live long; and Shanie was so upset that it took all three of us to bundle her into the car.

Luckily S is very good with dogs and, through that night, now has her own German Shepherd (odd things happen in odd ways at times). She sat in the back of my estate car with Shanie in her arms and tried to comfort her. To add to her woes, the poor bitch had been fed just before all the panic occurred and was very car sick.

We had taken a short cut to the Kennels as it's the other side of Caernarvon, to avoid the town, and the narrow winding lanes finished Shanie off. We had a very unhappy subdued bitch to hand over. Carol fed us with cocoa and we returned home, arriving around two in the morning.

Christine rang me at seven to say Jerry had died. She was on her own, having no relatives here and through her need to nurse Jerry all day and all night had not been able to make outside friends. I brought her home for the day and rang Hilary, who took Chris home for the weekend. She came to watch the performance at the cathedral where the dogs raised seventeen pounds by an on-the-spot sponsored downstay, people betting on the dog they thought would stay longest; they all did!

The club was marvellous. Chris went to stay with her parents for a week or so, Carol kennelled Shanie free, and when Chris returned we had had a whipround and she found flowers and groceries waiting for her. Shanie came back with a free sack of dogfood. Several members made a point of inviting Chris to visit them.

Her story has a very happy ending as a few weeks ago I called on her. She married again two years later and now has a little girl nearly two named Katie. Recently I went to see her new ten-day-old baby daughter, Lisa Joy. Shanie is still with her, now five years old and good with the children and the three cats, but as excitable as ever if people come, so I only heard her doing a Chita yodel; I didn't see her.

Hilary's story has had a different ending. Max became more and more of a responsibility; he was not only energetic but headstrong and he began to show signs of being dangerous too. Hilary, to her delight, after a number of years of marriage, discovered she was pregnant, but a dog like Max could, if he pulled her over, make her lose a much-wanted baby. She rang me up. What should she do?

I suggested the police. They jumped at the dog as he had had a very good background and also we had tried to train him; he knew some of the exercises required as a start to his future work; and he is now a working police dog and a very good dog indeed; but as energetic as ever, tough and powerful, in need of an experienced handler; not a dog for a novice.

Hilary couldn't bear the thought of life without a German Shepherd. This time she looked for an adult and found a dog that had been used at stud, but grown far too big for showing; his owners wanted a good pet home for him. Lordy was one of the last litter Mrs Charavigne ever bred and, like all her stock, is a big dog with a lovely nature. He is one of my longtime dogs, coming every week, except briefly while Hilary's little boy was a baby. She came back to club when Leslie was about eighteen months old, and has recently added to her menage. Leslie is four now.

She and Brian have bought a year-old Gordon Setter named Emma. Emma has never been

Chita practising her downstay. She is watching another dog in the distance and wants to get up and see him off.

In puppy class Hilary is explaining a point while the pups get used to a safe adult dog of their own breed.

A dog that refuses to lie still is a dog that can't be trained. The King Charles Cavalier and the Dobermann on the right are still playing up.

Now the King Charles Cavalier, Snoopy, has learned to lie still and behave.

Rudi was the first Dobermann to come to club. Like Chita, he is learning to track.

This is where Sally and I often meet when walking our dogs. In the distance is the Menai Straits suspension bridge.

Here little Sally is sitting correctly by Lordy who is six years old…

…but the temptation is too much. Lordy is not sure that he approves of six-month-old Sally's advances!

Chita practising an out-of-sight downstay in the Botanical Gardens. She can't see me but I can see her.

I am looking after Sally's Boxer, Susie, who behaved perfectly while I continued to teach. The dog is learning to stand still so he can be examined, by a vet if needed, without making a fuss.

Practising heelwork with Chita. She must sit in Trials heelwork every time I stop.

Spike the Rottweiler pup is learning to pay attention to his owner. He is doing it very well, waiting for a further command.

Sit at heel. Sally's Old English Sheepdog, Kim, is in a good position, but Goldie, the Retriever cross, has turned to look at her owner because Carol has turned her body.

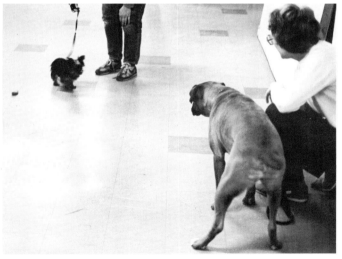

Penny, the Yorkie, is more interested in Susie, the Boxer, than in the toy mouse she is supposed to pick up.

Jamie

trained and Hilary is going to have fun! She is a delight of a dog, very lively, the opposite of Lordy who is very placid and finds humans as amusing as Puma did; Emma is full of love for the human race, an eager bitch that is a comic. They wanted another dog but decided a puppy would demand a lot of Hilary's time and also be a possible risk with a little boy of only four; puppies do not always grow into the kind of adults you want or hope for.

We have had two other Chita nephews in club. The first was a very tough dog indeed and his owner found him such a handful that she stopped coming. The dog became a major liability and bit several people before they at last realised they must take the ultimate unhappy step and say 'this is it'. He was put to sleep before he was two year old.

The other was Marcus, almost a duplicate of Max in every way. At five months old he knocked a child off his bicycle and became a major headache for Eirwen who owned him. He escaped from home and was killed by a car at eight months old. My only feeling was relief as Marcus was completely unmanageable; he was even worse than Max. To my pleasure Eirwen came back in September with an enchanting little German Shepherd bitch named Holly. Holly is now six months old and doing extremely well and Eirwen admits that Marcus's death was a mercy, as if he hadn't died she would almost certainly have had to put him down; he had all the signs of being a real villain.

Experienced breeders are getting away from this type of breeding. The dogs were bred on what is known as police dogs lines, but few police forces do have dogs bred for them. They take the dogs the public can't manage as they are like Marcus, and Max, and Chita, and the third Chita nephew. It is not normally even legal to advertise dogs bred for the police; they aren't. They got there because no one else could cope.

If you see an advertisement which says police-dog-type stock, find out which Force the dog is with and ask how they got him. It could be misrepresentation.

Those of us who run pet clubs know the misery caused by a dog that has to be put down, as, no matter how bad it is, it always finds a place in its owner's heart. It is rarely possible to live closely with any animal and not become fond of it. Usually, too, these animals behave well at home, alone with their owners. They have over-developed guarding instincts, which have not been channelled by training. It is only when visitors come to the house, or when taken out and meeting other people and dogs, that they become liabilities.

Whatever the reason, a biting dog can't be kept, and we know what the owners suffer. We help to hold the dog at the end, and offer its owner our shoulder to cry on. Come to think of it, we suffer too, as we knew the dog, and it was one of our failures. We tried our best and feel defeated.

Sometimes it is possible, if the dog is bold, to ask someone really reliable, like Eric Roberts, to take it on, train it and find it a good home; but if the dog is very nervous it can't be done. A nervous dog that bites is far more dangerous than a bold one. You might retrain the bold fellow; the nervous dog sees danger where none exists and defends itself against imaginary hazards.

Retraining for the owner, by someone else, only works if the owner will work on the dog when it returns. If the dog is allowed to revert to its old ways, then the training money has been wasted. Also there are a lot of cowboys in this game; it is essential to make very thorough enquiries before trusting a dog to someone who might be like the dog trainers I described in my book *Josse*. I have never met any like that, but there are some about; one reads of their prosecutions in the dog papers.

We now have eleven German Shepherds in the club, all with the most lovely temperaments. None is related to Chita. There are five dogs and six bitches, all bought from local breeders. Something has happened in the last few years to change the temperament and instead of dreading the breed, as I once did when new people enrolled, I am now enchanted by all of them.

A major factor in their control may be that new owners are bringing them to club as soon as they are inoculated, so that most of ours started at fourteen weeks old, and I can show people how to stop faults developing.

CHAPTER TEN

One of the more fascinating aspects of the club is that you never know quite what is coming through the door. Or what owners will do next! One of our club members who comes when she has young dogs to socialise is Barbara Swayne Williams. I knew her for years before I moved here as she has always had German Shepherds, is a judge of the breed and I met her when I was showing Puma.

She came to club first with Mecky, who is her stud dog, a lovely good natured animal. He is father of several of our present club German Shepherds. Mecky went on to do a lot of winning, and I was so used to Barbara as a stalwart of his breed that when she turned up in club next time I just stared.

She had bought a Saint Bernard. Jamie is the only one of *his* breed we have ever had in club and there came a point when I felt like saying, as in Alice during the court case, all dogs over nine miles high please stop coming!

Jamie is gorgeous and has also made his mark in the show ring. He is a huge amiable dog, but Chita is quite convinced he isn't a dog at all but a lion and goes into a blind panic when we meet unexpectedly. She did tolerate him in club, but obviously it took an effort to lie beside this giant animal. If Barbara and I could meet often we would soon get over this but we both work and we live twenty miles apart so it is impossible. She now also has two young dogs, Joker and Jester, Mecky sons, both beginning in their turn to do some winning.

Jamie is the dog on the cover of my book *All about Your Pet Puppy* which Pelham published some years ago. He was only a few months old then; he is much bigger now.

Our other really big dog, apart from an amiable Wolfhound that I fell for in a big way as like most of his breed he was so lovely in nature, was Oggi. Oggi is a Newfoundland and will be well known to a great many people who have enjoyed holidays at the Ogwen Bank Country Club caravan site, just outside Bethesda. He patrols, and amuses me immensely as one of the features of the site is the rabbits. Gwen Garner, who runs the place with her husband Alan, had some white rabbits which escaped and have interbred with the wild population. The place now has tame rabbits as an added attraction, which the children love.

Oggi saunters round, looking at rabbits, and at Gwen's cat, with a benevolent air and wouldn't dream of harming them. He is a really big animal and extremely handsome. I have postcards of him on my wall of fame, which is outside my study. It has about two hundred photographs of dogs; my own, my friends' dogs, dogs belonging to fans who send me their pictures; club dogs.

Gwen, Oggi's owner, was my first-ever private pupil; he taxed me to the limits as you can't put an enormous dog into position as you can the small ones, and Oggi has a mind of his own. He did train, and when I see him I am always reminded of his puppy days. When people come to me with small German Shepherd pups and say 'Oh, they are *lively*', I remember Oggi, aged about six months, standing behind his owner, on his hind legs, with his paws round Gwen's neck, while I tried every form of bribery and corruption I could think of to get him off. Liver worked; which meant he came off Gwen and crushed me against the wall!

Oggi is now a perfect gentleman, rather stately, and must be at least six years old.

Club nights now that everyone does come regularly are much happier for us all as the dogs are at the same stage and once they are under control we can be more ambitious and do much more interesting things with them.

For some years we held a sponsored downstay for a Guide Dog. We aimed at a penny a minute and a ten-minute down in position without the dog moving at all. The top dogs were off-lead, the others on-lead, and if we did this at an outdoor event we had the onlookers bet on the dogs; we managed to raise our £1,000 and named the dog Freya to commemorate a club dog that had died. Freya is a German Shepherd bitch that looks very like Chita. We were sent her photograph.

We are now starting to raise money for a second dog and are hoping to do another downstay. Chita, although she does not stay in place for ten minutes while I go out of sight in Trials because she is scared, has earned around £200 for sponsored downs, so she can do the exercise; maybe if she thought we were being sponsored at Trials she might stay there, but I am not sure the judges would allow it!

Puppy class is always rewarding. Few clubs have this as they consider it wrong to train puppies. We don't train them to a high degree; we have the owners sitting on the floor with the pups beside them, lying quietly, a safe big dog like Lordy, Hilary's German Shepherd, with them, to get them used to the room, the people and the dogs. As they get more confident they meet more dogs, learn how to sit, go down and lie still, and to stand to be groomed; and we do teach-ins on worms and fleas.

We also teach play-training with a toy so that the puppy runs to fetch it and bring it back and gets a tremendous fuss when it comes. I find it makes people much more confident when they start on the next course at six months as they haven't made mistakes I have to cure, and are at ease with their dog.

They learn to stop the puppy mouthing or nibbling them; how to house train correctly, as lots of people seem to get that all wrong and come with adult dogs that are still messy at night, usually through a misunderstanding of the way a dog is taught. The pup is taught to bring the owner everything it picks up and hand it over without being to possessive as this possessiveness is what can lead to real trouble and to a dog that bites to stop having its property taken off it, whether food or toy or a bone.

We try to help people play sensible games and not silly ones and to teach children what is play and what becomes, very quickly, torment that can end in them being bitten; to teach safe games for a child to play; hiding is one; hiding a dog toy is another; never chasing the dog as that teaches him to be a prize escaper from the hunter (you!) and he will never come; he has been taught to avoid coming.

He has to chase you; which is invaluable if your dog gets into a silly situation, as Chita did trying to help a family eat their picnic on the beach last November. Had it been summer I'd have leashed her, but it hadn't occurred to me someone might picnic on a beach we usually find deserted in wintertime. I just ran down the sands, she saw me running away, was afraid she'd lose me and chased after me; problem solved without a lot of yelling, shouting and frustration. Unfortunately they had been hidden from me by a sanddune, or I would have run off far more quickly and prevented the situation arising as they didn't really appreciate her interest; she did think they might have shared their food!

Not all puppies, unfortunately, prove ideal pets. One pup has caused me to jump speedily on anyone who says it's the handler not the dog, as this was an ideal and considerate owner who did her very best with what proved a more and more unhappy situation. The pup was a little Collie; and from the first he had a very strange look in his eyes and he growled at anyone who came near them.

No matter what we did, he refused to behave with people, and though he trained, the odd light never went from his eyes; he found the world very upsetting. I usually sit on the floor with pups; not too near, but at about three yards away, and either hold out a titbit or play idly with a toy. The vast majority become curious, come towards me and end up on my lap. Once they trust me I know I can help their owners without causing the puppy any fear, as I am now part of their lives and accepted, and they want my approval too.

This pup refused to approach me and would not allow anyone to approach him. The growls became more threatening week by week and I told the owner that I thought he had mental trouble. She loved him; he could be very sweet. The family had another older dog that behaved perfectly and showed no sign ever of any aggression.

By the time the pup began to mature I had to warn everyone to take very good care not to go anywhere near him; he menaced them all and the light in his eyes was very odd; a sort of glow that gave him a wild appearance. He learned his lessons and mostly behaved well.

We then had a talk from one of the police dog handlers who selected dogs for working. I asked his opinion and he came across after he had seen dog and owner to say he thought it had mental problems; had I told her? Yes. There was nothing either of us could do, and I worried in case the dog attacked her or her family or somebody outside.

Some weeks later Puma managed to pull a claw out, goodness knows how. I took her to the vet in the morning and was met as I got out of my car by the pup's owner, in considerable distress. He had attacked her husband the night before and they realised then that this was the end of the line. They had rung the vet who had agreed that he too thought the pup had a major brain problem.

She was too upset to take the dog in for his last injection, so I took him. It is not a task I care for, and nobody in the surgery does either; I have now been present when four club dogs have died, as well as holding Puma and past animals in my arms when put to sleep. It is the last thing any of us wants. It is, however, unavoidable and has to be accepted; nothing lives for ever.

I had thought maybe that was the end of our association but I had a phone call a week later to say they had heard of a litter of Golden Retriever pups. Did I know the breeder? I did and she is first-class. Would I go with them and help them choose? There was nothing I would like more, though I was determined not to help with the choice unless they picked a bad puppy.

They collected me and out we went to a charming house, with a lovely summer garden and the most enchanting Goldie bitch, a handsome beautifully mannered stud dog, quite unrelated to her, and two bitch puppies, both twelve weeks old and so alike it was difficult to choose.

The bitch watched amiably as the children played with the pups; the pups raced to us for petting, were bold, outgoing and thought humans the nicest things they had ever known. They played with a stick, they chased after a tossed hankie, they were absolutely delightful and I was very tempted to take whichever remained unchosen, but knew I would be most unpopular if I added a fourth dog to our menage.

We had already had several Goldies that came from the same place and had two with the stud dog as father but with different bitches as mothers, and every one was a success. In the end the children did a sort of eenie, meenie, minie, mo and picked their pet.

I thought she might fret on the way home, but not a bit of it. The car was lovely fun, we were lovely fun, the outdoors was lovely fun and her tail never stopped waving. She showed no signs of car sickness. We went to her new home and I went in for coffee. We showed pup the garden and invited her to spend at least a penny. She wanted to inspect her surroundings.

She sniffed round the kitchen, greeted the older dog, tried out her bed, then found a saucer of milk, drank it, bounded to the back door and barked. Let out, she spent a penny and barked to come in! I have never seen a pup like it. She was probably well taught by her mother as she was four weeks older than is normal but nobody had wanted a bitch; all the dogs had gone.

She came to club and trained easily; she was a total delight after their unhappy ten months with the Collie pup; she could be played with, walked, and was endlessly good-humoured. Sadly for me, her owner moved to too far a distance to come to club but occasionally I see a Golden Retriever bitch in the High Street, and as she catches my scent, she turns round and pulls back to me. Her owner stops and stares.

'Oh, it's you. I might have known,' as I renew my acquaintance with her lovely bitch.

That is another occasion when I know that the hours I give up that at times seem too fraught with despair because of lack of success, are really worth it, all the time, as to have dogs like this come to club and learn fast and go away to live out a very happy life with their owners is really what dog clubs are about.

CHAPTER ELEVEN

Sometimes the problems we get in club seem insoluble. Father dies and the family, with the kindest of intentions, buy mother a dog for company. Often they know nothing about dogs, so mother, who always seems to be tiny, lands up with an enormous Labrador, or a huge Boxer, or a Springer Spaniel, none of which is a suitable pet for an elderly lady with a first-time dog. The puppies are adorable; but that stage only lasts a few short months.

Sometimes mother doesn't even want a dog. She is free for the first time in her life and intended to have long holidays, visit friends and relatives, and now she can't, as she is more tied than ever before by the needs of a tiny helpless little animal.

The first thing to do in this case is to make absolutely certain mother does want a dog. An animal you don't want is worse than nobody at all, especially if, as these often do, it becomes out-of-hand and unmanageable.

When my father died, some years ago, my mother said she did want a dog. We made enquiries about several breeders and decided on a West Highland White. Lucky is small, manageable, an excellent guard dog in the house and she has been a hundred-per-cent success from the start.

Other breeds I would recommend for the elderly starting on a first-time dog are Shelties, Cavalier King Charles Spaniels and any of the breeds like Cairns or Corgis or Scotties. It is essential to make many enquiries as to the temperament of the stock, as every breed can have its villains and vice is inherited. A nervous bitch will have nervous puppies, unless they are taken from her at birth and given to a much more balanced animal to rear, so maybe the inheritance is not absolute. Genuine nervousness is inherited; I have seen that too often to be in any doubt. Chita has a nervous ancestor and many pups related to her are nervous in the same way.

Training overcomes it to a considerable extent, but few people understand how to use training to overcome nerves. Many who show in Obedience are using the ring to help gain the confidence of a nervous animal. I have seen a number performing very well, with owners who are working for the good of the dog and not aimed at top prizes.

The first eight weeks after birth is vital in the life of a pup. Pups brought up unhappily in a crowded noisy place show it. They need to be shown kindly that humans are nice to know, that other dogs won't harm them and that household noises are a fact of life, not terrifying sudden dins that they rarely meet. Unfortunately there are so many puppy farms catering for the people who don't make enough enquiries, buying on an inpulse, quite unaware that those pedigrees may tell a damning tale to a knowledgeable person. They may tell the reverse, but it needs a major disaster to make a caring breeder send pups to a dealer, a pet shop or a place that deals in dogs. The genuine breeder who loves his or her stock and is proud of its reputation may question you and decide you are not a suitable owner, and there will suddenly be no puppy for sale.

There is every chance that when people breed pups in large quantity those pups are badly fed, have worms and the kennels may well also have distemper and parvovirus. The bill of sale says 'no responsibility taken for pups after they leave these premises', and if I saw that I would refuse to buy. If the puppy is ill and dies in the night you are possibly as much as a hundred pounds to the bad; and too bad, you will be told you killed it by neglect. Upset by its death and the loss of your hopes for a good dog, you aren't in any state of mind to argue. You have an enormous guilt about something you can't possibly have done unless you stabbed it or beat it to death; it can't starve in twelve hours. I have known a number of people buy pups that died, within twenty-four hours, of distemper.

One of the saddest pups we had come to club was a young German Shepherd, aged about four months. He was thin, he hated humans and snapped at them and he was afraid of other dogs and snapped at them. The owner had been recommended to a kennels in one of the big cities, as breeding very good stock. What he didn't know and I did was that in fact this is a disguise for one of the biggest dog dealers in the country and we have had several from them, all unsatisfactory in one way or another, and of different breeds.

The owner was doing his best and was extremely unhappy. The dog needed hours of time spent on it to reassure it and socialise it. He hadn't hours to spare. I asked the history of the pup and he discovered it had not been bred in the kennels but two hundred miles away; it had been sent at six weeks old with a consignment of many pups, in a van right across the country. It was too young to leave its mother. It travelled in a confined space; it was undoubtedly car sick and distressed and would have been in a filthy mess when it arrived, possible not given even water on the way, as the people who do this are far from being caring people.

He was taken straight from the nest, rattled around, jolted, flung about in the cage, possibly sharing the cage with pups as frightened as he was, and then brought to an enormous place with rows of pens, put in a pen with other pups that would fight him and bite him and compete with him for food, fed by humans who were busy, perhaps rough and careless and had little time, as these places are always understaffed; they rarely pay good wages. He was bought at seventeen weeks; he looked much younger as he was so small. He had spent eleven weeks in a cage, belonging to no one, without knowing that humans had time for him, would be kind to him, would be gentle with him, and he did not intend to trust anyone.

After five weeks the owner rang to ask if I could find the pup a home; I won't, as nobody would thank me for wishing a major problem on them; I put him in touch with someone I knew but he wouldn't either; his reputation would suffer if he passed on such a pup. The owner left and I have never had the heart to find out the end of that story. I gave him the address of the German Shepherd Rescue Society; they have branches all over the United Kingdom. I suspect the pup is now dead, as there was no way anyone could have made up to it for those past weeks or proved to it that the world was a good place and not a wicked one; not without dedicating himself day and night to the pup for weeks. He had paid one hundred and fifty pounds for it, but when I saw the pedigree it certainly was not worth anything like that amount.

Another owner did dedicate herself to her rescued animal. Her dog had been battered as a young dog and she got it from the RSPCA at two years old. He was a miserable-looking animal, a big lean Collie with the wildest look in his eyes I have ever seen. She had had him a fortnight when she joined us, to try and socialise the dog. Training was impossible at that stage.

We couldn't move too near him; we couldn't even lift a hand without him crouching on the floor, his eyes terrified. It took three weeks for him to accept me near him and another two before I was able to stroke him, never with a hand that came from a natural position, but crouched on the floor to make myself small and tickling his chest. By the end of term he would lean against me and accept that chest tickle.

By the end of term, too, he would heel-walk beautifully and work with other dogs so long as no men were near him. We couldn't lift dumbbells, or for that matter at first even a pen, if he were near; we had to watch how we approached him, never fast or carelessly. His owner is wonderful with him, and prepared to reassure him quickly if someone does something silly or someone else picks up a possible weapon, in his eyes, (which could even be a slipchain which could be thrown) when they are near. A lead held casually in the hands could be used to thrash a dog, so nobody could take a lead and hold it near him.

One day I brought a hurdle to give the dogs a change; he wouldn't come into the room with that strange object there; it scared him nearly witless and I had to remove it quickly and lie it on the floor. He did sniff at it, very anxiously, but we did not put it up; there was no point in frightening him unnecessarily as he is not going to compete in shows, and it is important that he should accept his normal environment. Club is helping him accept people and dogs and he came in towards the end of the last session with a waving tail. His eyes no longer have that terrified look, unless we do something unusually stupid; if someone rushes at him and waves a lead then he reverts and we have to calm him.

It is very difficult to make some people, especially those with happy friendly easy dogs, understand that all dogs are not exactly like theirs. People like that give me major problems with Chita. She was bitten badly by a stray dog at sixteen weeks; she was chased three times round Charlie Wyant's field on one of his courses by a big grey sable German Shepherd bitch. She distrusts Collies as it was a stray Collie that bit her, and she bristles at all big sables.

She has improved, as yesterday I went over to a small group of people who want to do Working Trials, mainly to socialise Chita and practise her stays. I explained what I needed to the trainer. He and his wife compete in Working Trials and he knew exactly what I needed and trains the same way as I do.

We arrived late as it was Armistice Sunday and I was held up by bands of people marching to Church (making me feel guilty) and then, although I had a splendid map, the road I needed was closed; the diversion didn't go in the right direction and I was lost.

The first thing I was asked to do (in a very large outdoor area) was heelwork with another German Shepherd owner. The other dog started his heelwork by attacking Chita; I sat her fast (she was leashed), the trainer took the dog and to my pleasure she didn't retaliate. She behaved beautifully all morning, in spite of several dogs getting loose and chasing each other past her, and, even when off-lead, came back to me at once the only time she was tempted to run towards another dog.

It's been a long hard road; and we haven't ended it by any means.

But with Working Trials, unlike Obedience, there is always another advance to be made: longer tracks, older tracks; better control and longer sendaways; improving the dog all the time so that as you and the dog learn to team together, you do become a partnership, and not two beings who live together for convenience, one hoping desperately for a companionship that is never achieved, the other staying because mostly it's to its convenience as there is food there and warmth there and an owner that will allow the dog to do exactly as it pleases, whether that is a good idea or not.

I could never have lived with Chita on those terms;

she would have been put down by now as she would
have been impossible to own.

CHAPTER TWELVE

I not only come across problems with dogs in clubs, but my post brings me in numerous letters each week, most of them to do with dog matters. Many people who have read the two books on Chita (*Three's A Pack and Two for Joy*) have been reassured to find someone else does have a dog like theirs.

I have kept all the letters, as it is useful to go back and read about a behaviour problem that I might meet in club. Others deal with inherited problems, and with pancreas deficiency, in *Two's Company*, which was about Janus and his bad hips and his peculiar inside.

Most breeders care very deeply about inherited faults and do their best to avoid them. Nobody can be one hundred per cent successful. Livestock isn't like that. Babies can be born with Downe's Syndrome or congenital hip deformities too.

I wrote about Janus's bad hips and incurred a lot of hostility from some breeders. Many backed me, and wrote to say I need never show Golden Retrievers as long as I live, as the breeders would see that I never won. I was too upset at the time by owning a dog with a bad fault who was in considerable pain, to do anything about it, but I wish now I had kept that letter as the writer should have been reported. Now, ten years later, I don't even remember her name. I burned the letter in disgust.

Today many breeders X-ray their stock. The fault is common in most of the big breeds. If it is not too bad the dog can live with it, as Janus has for thirteen years, with nothing more than occasional arthritis now to trouble him, but it is a disaster in a working dog. The dog is simply not capable of the demands made on him, so that it is important for all of us who are doing Working Trials to make sure we do buy stock from breeders who take good care, or we will be unable to continue with our hobby. I bought Janus for Trials. I wouldn't get rid of my dog just for my benefit, to buy another for Trials; I had bought him, so for seven years I was unable to compete other than in Obedience, which isn't nearly so interesting, as he wasn't able to jump, and Puma wasn't suitable; she couldn't scale. She was a heavy bitch and had had a litter before I tried to teach her to jump.

Some of the writers wrote again and I was able to follow up what happend to the dogs. Others wrote for advice and I never did hear if it helped. I don't give veterinary advice; only on management of the dog.

Three dogs in particular are memorable, as their owners kept in touch while the dog was being treated. I send them a letter which they can take to their vet before they begin on my suggestions. Thirteen years of managing Janus's inside and keeping it working perfectly has given me a lot of practical experience in both sickness and health of the dog. Chita has the same complaint but to a much less degree. Puma had no sign of it. I had never heard of it until it was diagnosed in Janus. It is becoming more common, though no one knows why.

The first of the dogs I was told about was William, a flat-coated Retriever; the second was Sam (short for Samantha) a young German Shepherd; the last dog was not named by the writer, though she gave a hilarious description of its behaviour, which was her problem, not pancreas trouble.

William's owner rang me one Christmas Eve almost in tears, having determinedly tracked down my name and phone number. William had all the typical symptoms, the appalling diarrhoea, the gauntness and the wildness and she thought he might not live much longer.

I kept notes of Janus's rehabilitation, and once earned myself deep undying hatred from someone who didn't read on in an article because I said I experimented with his diet. The reader promptly thought I meant vivisection though why you should cut up a dog to feed him was beyond my understanding, though not it turned out, beyond hers. So far as she was concerned I was the devil in human disguise, making my poor dog's life a misery!

I told William's owner about my experiments. Quite simply, I tried various things to see if I could get weight on Janus as one of the most distressing symptoms is extreme thinness and busybodies instead of asking if you have seen a vet immediately report you to the RSPCA for starving the dog. Someone did it to me; I had a very angry vet, fortunately, who flew to my defence.

Someone else took it on himself to tell me off in dog club, when Janus was young, for starving my dog and being too mean to buy meat; my vet bills ran, in 1973, at about thirty pounds a month and Janus had about £2 a day spent on him; his food ran straight through him.

I have someone in club now with a dog that has a nasty-looking injury due to an injection that went wrong; it does look dreadful, as there is a raw patch and a deep sore, not surprisingly since needles go in deep, and it is being treated, but no end of people assume she is too lazy to go to the vet! Or too mean. Why people are so self-righteous and so quick to judge without evidence I can't think.

I now make sure that these things come into the open so that there won't be gossip, having suffered it myself. People have so many different viewpoints and can be quite sincerely convinced they are right and others are wrong. Those who let their dogs out to roam are sure they are doing right and think those of us who keep them in are cruel and don't let the dog do what comes naturally. No one will ever convince them they are wrong, till the dog lies dead under a car, or shot in a sheepfield, or vanishes having been picked up and sold to an illicit vivisection group. They pay well.

I finally managed to get Janus up to weight by giving him five meals a day, all small, with his added pancreas extract on it, supplied by the vet. Experiments showed he did better on five than on three meals. I also experimented with quantities; less meat and more biscuit; bran; weighing everything until I found a mixture that suited him, that produced nice firm stools which are a diagnostic part of this complaint, and then, with baby dinners added carefully, he began to put on weight.

I had a phone call from William's owner four months later. She was over the moon as she had shown my letter to her vet and they had experimented with William's diet. When she rang he was a fit dog with a shining coat and extremely active. That is one of the most rewarding experiences I have ever had through my books.

There have been others, but not everyone writes to tell me whether or not the dog did improve. Among the very few that have written afterwards are Sue and Tony Sleet who said I could use their experiences to help other owners.

The bitch is a young German Shepherd named Samantha.

Sam had the typical symptoms, the thinness, lack of concentration, diarrhoea. The trouble is that every dog varies in its response to treatment and what suits one in the way of food won't suit another. That does have to be a matter for experiment, done very carefully and under veterinary supervision.

Even an ounce or two too much or too little or the wrong balance can make a difference. I weigh everything for my dogs when they eat anyway, or they would be over or underfed. They don't have the same food, as Chita's doesn't suit Janus; he now is almost thirteen and has had two bad attacks of nephritis so he lives on a nephritis diet which has to come from the vet. It does suit him very well indeed.

Sue commented in her last letter that Sam now weighs 63 lbs and is very lively and active. She has many of Chita's characteristics; races wildly if let off lead, as Chita did at first; she is much more controlled and sensible now and behaves like a more normal dog.

Sue has the same trick phrase as I have: 'Sam, BEHAVE.' Sam loves to jump for a tin can on command, or on the counter-command of LEAVE IT she ignores it, which is excellent training for any dog, as to stop doing something they love is real control and it is not cruel as it leads on to stopping them chasing dogs or cats or sheep.

Sue commented that the sight of a GSD pounding over the field, flying in the air towards her, gives some people heart attacks and one man yelled 'look out' when Sam was behind Sue and leaping at her. Sue said NO and Sam sailed by without touching her.

People with small dogs rarely think of ours as being just a small dog on a larger scale and equally bouncy and happy; those racing at the owners are indulging in a loving greeting and a licked face, not attacking them!

When Sue took Sam back to the vet for a checkup he thought she had a new dog. This was after trying my advice, so I was as thrilled as Sue and Tony. Sam has steroids, which Janus has never had, but his treatment started ten years ago and far more is known now. The disability is wretchedly common and no one knows why.

Steroids can have side-effects.

Sam does well on a fish diet, but this may not be right for every dog; some do well on a diet of brains; others of an all-purpose food; others on well-known dog foods, though as the dog doesn't digest meat a diet very high in protein seems unwise.

Many people think of a dog with this disorder as being an invalid. One of my step-grandsons has severe diabetes; it is also a disorder of the pancreas and we all take his two injections a day for granted and never think about them. He leads a very normal life, and does not consider himself disabled.

Nor does Janus. In spite of arthritis in his hips which makes him stiff at times, he walks (very slowly) about two miles a day and is most put out if I go out with Chita and don't take him. He enjoys long walks with Kenneth on the beach, where in the last week he has found about six balls and chased two rabbits! Janus running at slow stately lollop after a speeding rabbit needs to be seen to be believed, but he is convinced he can catch it, ultimately. He gives up when he is out-of-breath which is fairly soon as he lives now also on heart pills.

His deafness gives Kenneth problems as my husband doesn't believe in leads. He would if he ever tried to take Chita out. Her turn of speed is amazing and she is out of sight very fast indeed; the result is I exercise total control all the time as she does not like other dogs barking at her. She never has bitten any dog, but I am not going to find out the hard way whether or not she would.

Recently husband and old dog went off together for a beach walk while I took Chita tracking. The beach walk for some obscure reason turned into a forest walk. Janus found a wonderful smell in a bramble thicket and in he went. It was a very large thicket and Kenneth, somewhat to his annoyance, found himself unable to follow, unable to see the dog and quite baffled as to just what he should do, as calling Janus produces no effect. He just does not hear. He knows what a mouth saying cheese means; he can lip-read that and so people often think we are wrong and he can hear.

No sign of Janus and there is Kenneth squatting absurdly peering into the brambles feeling a fool. JANUS. Nothing happened. After five minutes Kenneth stood up, wondering if he could go round the thicket and see if the dog was on the other side. He turned round. Janus was sitting watching him peer into the thicket, just behind him, his mouth open in amusement, obviously enjoying the sight of his master enduring a private moment of worry all because of a stubborn old dog.

Needless to say, when I got home he said: 'You and your so-and-so dog!'

I didn't really soothe his feelings as I thought it extremely funny. I have been caught out by that habit of Janus's myself, so often. I keep him on a long line; he can't wander away then or chase rabbits and possibly drop dead somewhere inaccessible to me. Nobody could regard him as an invalid – he is quite unaware of all his various complaints and ignores them.

Letters from readers who have dogs cheer me immensely as others do suffer too in the same ways! One fairly recent letter was from someone who had three easy dogs of the same breed in twenty-four years and then was persuaded to take on another dog. Number four, though of a different breed, was another Chita. This isn't surprising as the working breeds if bred hard on working lines are exceptionally active animals.

This reader is someone after my own heart as she comments that, though harmless, a large black dog hurtling to leap on someone not used to dogs can be remarkably frightening. So they must be trained for control.

They had gone to look after animals for friends

going on holiday. She describes their arrival:

'There was a horrendous hurtling crash and a yowl that sounded like the Hound of the Baskervilles from somewhere inside. Much shouting and door slamming and we were invited to come in "if we thought we could bear it".'

The noise proved to be due to an untimely and inappropriate present. The donor had not realised that the owners were now unable to cope with a new puppy and the writer of the letter to me found herself agreeing to take the pup home at the end of their stay.

She commented that during the three weeks she began to wonder as they live in a small home, though in country surroundings. The pup never stopped tearing round from morning till night. She goes on:

'This black demon was intent on only one thing, apart from the ritual food, of course. Tear around like a lunatic, grab anything that was not nailed down — and I *do* mean anything, like armchairs (never mind cushions), sidetables, the bannisters, pull the knob off the front door (Victorian brass and huge), pull up the stair carpet, grab every towel in the house.'

She also shrieked in the car, roared at every car that came near her and leaped like a kangaroo in both horizontal and vertical directions. She was one year old, underweight (she would be with all that nervous energy) and never stopped moving till she collapsed in an exhausted heap.

J had to learn anew how to cope with a dog as none of her others had been in the least like this. This was a boss dog; a Chita type, a dog that was not going to take any notice of *any* human. She had no intention of learning; no intention of listening; and she didn't mind being bawled at as that was all her other owners had ever been able to do with her.

One day J had a brainwave and said 'Dinner?' in a whisper. A very puzzled dog looked at her. It worked. The lunatic dog learned fast. She got *nothing* until she SAT without fussing.

Like all these animals, she had saving graces. (It would be easy if they were utterly horrible, but they never are.) She craved affection, as most of these do. Chita does, and will ask for it from anyone. So many people dislike her riotous method of greeting them which, though well-controlled, can still alarm those who don't like dogs, so that those who do like her are greeted with total fervour. This, of course, adds to *my* problems as she can't at first distinguish between those who like her and those who are going to loathe her; those who like her encourage her bad behaviour, and I can't correct her as they get so hurt, sure I am suffering from jealousy and don't want my dog to like them!

This pup never destroyed anything though she grabbed it, and she was anybody's dog if they offered food. This again seems to be a characteristic of this type of dog. Chita could once easily be bribed and at one Trial I had great difficulty in controlling my temper with an onlooker as Chita fled past me during one of the exercises and disappeared into the crowd. I found her and asked the woman she was with why Chita had gone to her.

'I had some sausages I didn't much like; so I gave them to her and she was eating them while you were waiting and she saw I still had one left,' said the culprit, quite unaware of the fact that she had just cost me about twenty points.

The black pup that behaved like Chita had to learn unexpectedly fast as J became extremely ill and went in to hospital four weeks after their return home with the dog. By the time she came out the kangaroo leaps had been curbed and the pup knew the word SIT. J's husband had worked extremely hard as an out-of-hand dog is a major hazard with an invalid in the house.

This happened four years ago and black dog is now angelic by comparison though, like Chita, far from perfect. Now they can say 'yes' when the dog says 'I'm a good girl, aren't I?' instead of 'yes, I did crash through that door and so what?'.

Like Chita, she still needs lessons but those, like ours, are fun; she needs loads of exercise and lots of things to do as she bores easily. Her owners, like me, are never bored. We may be frustrated or irritated or ripe for murder, but never, never bored.

CHAPTER THIRTEEN

I started training Janus for Obedience twelve years ago. I was taught, for eleven and a half years of his life, by those who compete in Obedience only and not in Working Trials. All those who taught me said more or less the same about Chita.

Get on top of that bitch.

Make her behave.

Show her who's boss.

I had some control over her; she would obey me, mostly; every now and then that dominance flared and I saw in her what I see every week in my new young club dogs: a wilful desire to have her own way at all costs, and a cunning that could outwit me whenever she chose.

She is an utter little swine, said one of my police dog handler friends, after she had been let off lead and attacked all his grown police dogs. She was five months old at that time.

She's all bitch, said another of my teachers, battling with Chita, forcing her to do as he wanted. That day, Chita bit. She objected to an almost stranger forcing her.

Every instinct told me something was wrong. I had brief glimpses of what I wanted during a weekend in which I stayed with Irene and John Cree, when Chita was only a year old. I read the manuscript of John's bood before it iwas published and had got to know him then. The copy I have (it has now been retitled *Training the German Shepherd Dog* and was *Training the Alsatian*) has nearly fallen apart. I have read it so often.

It began to show me what was wrong, but books don't teach you everything. John has a different approach to the Obedience people. It wasn't possible, in two days, to isolate it and utilise it. All I did realise was that he does teach differently.

Sheila Hocken, whose Guide Dog Emma became so famous in a recent edition of the pet owner companion magazine to *Dog Training Weekly*, which is titled *The Companion Dog*, writes about dog clubs. She says that some of them are good; others are absolutely diabolical. (That is her word, not mine.) She makes the comment too that the newcomer is bound to believe the instructor, and that it is quite frightening to think that anyone can set up a dog club. She adds that in her experience some of the instructors don't even appear to like dogs, let alone understand them.

This was my experience too and time after time when I asked why an exercise was done, I was told for the good of the dog. It makes it behave.

I needed knowledge with both Janus and Puma, but I never got what I needed from anyone, or from any book. Half the instructors I met were competition people who told me to put mine down and get easy dogs.

What sort of advice is that?

I became more and more demoralised, doubting my own ability; wondering if the fact that I tried to understand the dog was detrimental to training. I wanted to use the professionalism I had learned in writing to find out about training dogs. There had to be more than I was being told.

There had to be a reason for all those exercises, perhaps lost in the past; they hadn't been devised for competition; they had been devised to obtain control.

I had a brief frustrating conversation with Captain Philip Gurney, one of the old-timers, at a show, during which he told me that when he and others first devised competitions they did not envisage the path which has been taken. It was originally to test whether or not handlers could control their dogs; not to test a precision that can only come from a strain of dog that hadn't then been bred.

The winning dogs today have been carefully selected by breeding programmes for the most part. There are some that haven't, but they also are very exceptional dogs. Muriel Pearce's words heartened me. I have been learning on dogs that many top handlers would sell or put down. I have taught them; they don't shine; but that isn't entirely because I am a bad handler. My story would have been very different if I had bought easier dogs, or if I had lived near people like Karina Smith, who has won Crufts and has also made her bitch into a dual champion in Obedience and Working Trials; or Charlie Wyant, who has lost count of the number of champions he has help train and has had at least four himself; and Sylvia Bishop, another born instructor whose dogs do both Trials and Obedience.

I met Wendy Volhard whose Newfoundlands have become Obedience champions in the States. She was here on a visit. I again had a tantalising glimpse of a different way of training. That was only a day's meeting; I wrote to her and got a further glimpse, but that isn't enough.

I began to feel like one of King Arthur's questing knights; on and on in search of something you have just glimpsed round the corner, but never reached.

I went on one of Roy Hunter's courses and it happened again. A different approach; a more relaxed approach, reminding me of John Cree. I wanted to know more, but there was only a week and I was one of a group, and though I tried hard to pinpoint the difference in his approach, I didn't get there. His methods are gentle. He trained police dog handlers and their dogs for the Metropolitan police from 1958 until 1981. So if he used gentle methods, then the police he trained did too, and they are a very successful Force.

I had some fascinating conversations with Roy at lunchtime in the pub and we are now friends. He came up this year to judge my club. I wouldn't have dared ask him two years ago. His writeup was in the same issue of *Companion Dog* as Sheila Hocken's piece on dog clubs.

He starts by saying he was a little concerned by my request as if he disagreed with the way I taught he would have to say so in all honesty. In fact he says that he need not have worried as it was obvious from the start that though some of our methods differ, we both have the same principle of inducive training (where possible) and never putting the dogs under stress.

It is a very rewarding writeup.

But two years ago I needed to know more. I wasn't being successful in club; it wasn't disastrous but I was sure I could do far better if I found the key to unlock the knowledge I needed. People left; people didn't try; people didn't seem to make progress. Chita was still defiant at times, though far better than ever before. I went to Trials with her; succeeded in some of the exercises, but we still didn't know nearly enough about tracking. That's easy when you lay the track and know where it is, but to go out on a big field without an idea where the track is, and leave it all to the dog, is very daunting indeed.

I did gain more knowledge, but it wasn't exactly what I needed. Many Trials consist mostly of police dog handlers and their dogs. Devon last year had twenty-six police dogs and twenty civilian dogs. I picked the police brains about tracking. They do it for real. They are also always extremely kind and helpful and I usually find I do much better under police judges than under those who have been brought in from the Obedience world for the control exercises.

At Tatton Trials two years ago, feeling defeated, as Chita had just done a beautiful track, not on the tracklayer's trail but on a deer trail, I went to buy leads to sell in club and talked to the man who ran the equipment stall. I was fed up with struggling alone; I couldn't teach myself. I didn't understand enough about the techniques or the way the dog worked. All I got from Obedience people when I asked for tracking help was: 'I have my own ideas about tracking.' Which was no use and merely masked the fact that my informant had no experience either.

I told him how I felt. I seemed to spend all my time helping other people and getting no help from anywhere myself.

'Why don't you go and see Eric Roberts after the Trials? He's Trials Manager. I think he is the man you need.'

I did go, and made an appointment to go over to Macclesfield for a lesson. He is a brilliant instructor. In that hour things became plain to me that had not been plain before; and I knew that though I had been taught all about training a dog, much of which I could utilise, but in an entirely different way, nobody had ever taught me anything about *handling* a dog.

I did know it, up to a point; I have never gone along with the idea that you teach all dogs at the same speed, in a group, by the same method, as that most certainly does not work. A fast German Shepherd, large and lively, owned by a twenty-year-old man, is in a group of people that also contains a tiny Jack Russell, a crossbred that has been rescued and is apt to bite and old Mrs Smith who is well over seventy, has arthritis in her feet and a Springer Spaniel dragging her around. Put all those on the floor together, say 'Forward' and the result is utter chaos.

I only once did mass heelwork with Chita when,

in her early days, friends took me to their club down south. I was told off for giving my pup a very hard corrective check; she was only five months old. What the instructor didn't know was that by the time I got her back to me she had a mouth full of fur which I pocketed hastily and guiltily, hoping no one else had noticed! If I hadn't checked her she would have had a great deal more than fur, as she is triggered so easily to chase and the sight of that bounding animal in front of her was more than she could stand. I decided to take her outside to spend a penny after that, and didn't join that exercise ever again with her anywhere.

I don't do mass heelwork in the lower classes in my club. The dogs round the room practise lying still while one dog at a time works at heeling on a loose lead. That way I can move the slow dogs fast and the fast dogs more slowly, as a fast dog going fast gets out of control and a slow dog going slow comes to a standstill eventually.

It is possible to do mass heelwork with highly trained dogs under total control and it looks beautiful done properly.

I have had six lessons from Eric. He has trained police dogs in Dubai and Tanzania, and is able to make things very clear. What I had to do with Chita was to change my entire approach; play with her much more, and as she did get out of control, then use the training she had had to get her back in control, but not by pressure. If she was played with, she would be more cooperative.

I had been told not to play with her before, or let her riot ever as she would get completely out of hand. I did play with her as I do with my dogs, but rather guiltily!

Now her whole attitude has changed. Boy, this is *fun*. We had it in jumping and the search before but never in heelwork.

Somehow in those few hours I began to

understand what I was doing and why. Better still, I knew what I was doing wrong in club. The dogs we had were mostly easy dogs and that approach of make the dog do it, was all wrong. I still needed to find out more about teaching in club. My six lessons with Chita had made so much difference to both of us that person after person was commenting on her changed attitude to me.

The look in her eyes is soft; she is submissive now in a way she never was before and the days of defiance are very rare indeed. Furthermore, with that changed attitude I could take her to places that I would never have dared to have taken her to a year before, and spread my wings in a way that also hadn't been possible before.

Mostly, when we went on publicity events to schools and other places, or stayed in hotels, I had to make very sure I did have control over her. Now she was cooperating with me and behaving because she wanted to please me.

She is never dangerous, but she is an enthusiastic dog and it is necessary, always, to make sure that nobody pets or fusses her as then she will leap at them trying to lick their faces. Her leaps are very forceful. One of them knocked my hand, five years ago, against the hatchback edge of my car and I had to have three stitches in my knuckle; another, a year later, greeting her dearly loved friend, our vet, nearly broke his nose. It took him several minutes to recover from the bang her hard skull had given him. We weren't popular that day!

Now, before she has any training, she has a game. I can do all sorts of things with her that I couldn't even a few months ago. Somehow, those lessons with Eric and my conversations with Muriel had stood all I had learned on its head and I realised what training was about, and why the competition exercises were devised. In class we practise the exercises and I tell everyone their uses, and why we do them, and now people see a reason, they can utilise the control commands at home and when out, and achieve far better results.

It is essential to be very clear when teaching. I found confusion in someone recently over one of the more vital exercises. This is the American long down and its use is described extremely well in Joachim Volhard and Gail Tamases Fischer's book, *Teaching Your Dog*, which is coming over here from Howell Book House in the USA. Wendy Volhard, who is Joachim's wife, sent me a copy.

The long down is to teach the dog that you are the master; the topdog; and keep him in a submissive position for half an hour. This soon changes his attitude to you. One club member told me she had stopped doing it as the dog enjoyed it and so it was no longer a punishment!

It was never intended as a punishment, but as a way of exerting control and making the dog understand he must do it when you ask. Once he begins to enjoy it and accept it, it must be kept up, though not every day, as a reminder you are stronger and have a stronger will than he. But you have achieved a major victory; the dog likes being told what to do!

Roy told Spike the Rottweiler's owner to use it to achieve mastery; you can't prove in many ways that you are the stronger than a dog that size, as you are not. All you have is low cunning to persuade him you are top dog and not he. It has had a very good effect. Spike is much more biddable. He wasn't vicious; just rather awkward and if he wanted to sleep against the china cupboard and prevent people from having plates to eat on, then sleep against it he did!

So I have now to make sure people understand training isn't punishment; the whole attitude is that dog and owner work together and enjoy being together as partners; the dog a junior partner and not the boss, doing as he wishes and forcing his owner to obey his slightest whim!

All breeds, except for the real Lapdogs, were bred to work. Poodles were hunting dogs and the Standard Poodle is a gundog in the United States; they need to work to feel good, and are no more happy lying around than is a man who is unemployed.

The destructive dog is a bored dog. Train him and the destruction stops. Fail to give a Retriever his 'pheasant' and he may end up biting in frustration. The training is a substitute for work and gives the dog a feeling of wellbeing and enormous pleasure. It produces the sort of dog that Chita has become, as I was to find out when I spread my wings with her in a totally different direction to any that I had taken in past years.

CHAPTER FOURTEEN

'Once I was marooned in Market Drayton...'

I said it without thinking, as the start of a sentence intended to recount something that happened to me there. I was in the Committee Room at the Hayes Conference Centre at Swanwick, as one of the ten guest speakers invited there during the week of the Writers' Summer School.

There were over three hundred writers there; some very well known indeed, some just starting on their careers. It was my first visit. Others had been coming for years.

It is a kind of Mecca for writers. During the week there are lectures, discussion groups and various courses, which during my visit ranged from how to write detective stories to a series of talks on graphology (the science of handwriting).

I had been invited in the spring by Mike Legat, who is himself the author of *Dear Author, A Writer's Guide to Publishers* and, among other fiction novels, *Mario's Vineyard*. I knew little about Swanwick at the time, although I knew of its existence. I was not at all sure what happened there.

I have known Mike since 1966. He was then one of the directors of Transworld Publishers, and he bought paperback rights of *The Running Foxes*, my first book for adults. It was published under the Corgi imprint and I have had a long and happy association with both Corgi and Carousel (their children's imprint) ever since.

During my own talk, which was the last of the ten

main lectures, at eight o'clock on the last night (giving me plenty of time to hatch a million butter-flies inside me) I told everyone how *The Running Foxes* had been sent first to Duttons in the United States as an entry for their animal award book.

I received a curt letter which I have kept and which is now in a scrap book.

'Dear Sir,
Your book is not of the calibre we expect.
Sincerely...'

I wrote it because I have seen foxes when out walking, watched them from hides and been fascinated by them all my life. It is not a fox story; it is not a hunting story. It is the story of an old man and his dog, and of the men who kept hounds and hunted with them.

I was not in the least surprised by Duttons' reply. Rejection is a way of life for new authors. One gets used to it! I put the book away in a cupboard. That seemed such a waste that one afternoon I went down to the library and went through the shelves. Who did publish that kind of book? I came up with Peter Guttman, the owner of a small hardback publishing firm called Hammond, Hammond and Co. He had published *The Egg and I*, which is one of the funniest books about the countryside I have ever read.

I sent the book to him and within two weeks, which is, I now realise, an incredibly short time, had an offer for the book from him. Life suddenly became unreal, as I was invited to London; my children were then still children and still at home; but I managed to go up, in a horrible suit that was all I had, as I live in slacks, and jerseys, or blouses, being too busy out-of-doors for more conventional attire.

I was so nervous that I didn't know if I could cope with a meal in a first-class London restaurant. I can't even remember now where we met, except that it was off Leicester Square and I walked down a street full of sex shops and was rescued by a policeman, as I realised I had blundered into quite the wrong district!

Peter was overwhelming; he spoke with a strong German accent and he kissed my hand; he loved my book and treated me like royalty, which was the only time that ever happened to me. He owned an enormous Airedale that was very definitely his boss! The dog pulled him everywhere and the only way he could get it to go down was by bellowing at it in an astonishing voice.

There followed a halcyon period that now seems like a dream. The book was published and acclaimed; it was sold all over the world, with Duttons, who had refused it, among the bidders, which rather delighted me. It was serialised; it was sold in America to Viking Press, and life became even more unreal.

The unreality only lasted for a few weeks, as the book was published in November and Peter died of a coronary very early in January. This for a very new author, was devastating, especially as the firm was taken over by Barrie Rockcliffe, who had my second book, *Breed of Giants*. It was not their kind of book, but had already been bought by the firm before the takeover.

Between them Mike Legat and Ed Cork and his daughter Pat, who are still my agents, kept me from giving up writing. Pat also had a Golden Retriever; and I got to know hers very well; she was entirely responsible for my purchase of Janus a few years later, after Kym, our Siamese cat died. There had been no way we could keep Kym and a dog.

My career as a countryside writer and writer about animals has been enormously helped by the fact that almost every one of my editors and my publishers as well as my agents has one, two or more dogs or cats, or both. Mike too has a Golden Retriever, Comus, who is three years younger than my Golden Retriever, Janus, so when we don't talk about books we talk about dogs.

So Mike had come back into my life. We had had no contact for some years except for a Christmas card, as he has left Transworld and is a full-time author, working, as I do, at home. It would be lovely to meet him again. We are both too busy to visit one another. I wrote to say I would love to go to Swanwick, but what on earth could I do with Chita? Janus is fine, staying at home with Kenneth, but this six-year-old German Shepherd bitch, though now a very well behaved and highly trained animal, is not always good with other people, and she frets for me.

I have only tried to kennel her once, when my car broke down at a friend's kennels. She screamed for ten minutes and when I went to her her mouth and claws were bleeding where she had tried to break her way out. The two older dogs, as Puma, my older German Shepherd, was alive then, were watching her in amazement. Even their presence did not comfort her.

I wrote to tell Mike I would love to come, but I just couldn't leave Chita.

I soon received another letter to say Chita could come too.

So here we were: there were no other dogs and Chita was in her element, the only dog among over three hundred people. I had to ask everyone not to fuss her as she is a petting addict. Some dogs pester for titbits; once Chita has been stroked, she pesters for affection. If everyone stroked her, I might well be suddenly pulled down stairs, as she tried to reach a dear newmade friend.

The world was made for Chita; and so were people. Those who don't try and control her are twisted round her paws, very sweetly, and inveigled by her into doing things I don't allow, like letting her climb on beds, or leap up with muddy paws and dirty a clean white shirt.

A concourse of writers is like nothing else as we all invent; we pick up ideas and toss them and at one time I found myself plotting an absurd mystery with Vivian Stuart, the author of the Australian series which includes *The Exiles* and *The Explorers*; on another occasion I was sitting with someone, whose name I don't know, inventing the scenario for a thriller, and no matter what anyone said, somebody was promptly busy turning it into an article or a book.

Ideas float round; heads are put together, conversations cause ideas to flourish and Swanwick must trigger many new books. It was responsible for making Lilian Daykin, a friend of mine for many years, who died some years ago when she was over 90, into a children's author. Among its regulars is also Mary Wibberley who will be well known to readers of romantic novels. Mary gave us a hilarious talk entitled 'A funny thing happened on the way to the Ritz'. A great many funny things happened; and the Ritz was not her usual location.

So it wasn't really surprising that my casual sentence should provoke the response: 'That's a super first line for a book!' We were all very conscious of first lines because Mike, who is chairman, and who kept everyone in gales of laughter, had invented a game for us.

He introduced the main speakers, one in the morning from 10 until 11, and one in the evening from 8 until 9. Before each one spoke Mike produced a first line from a well-known book and asked for us to guess title and author. One was the first line of *Pride and Prejudice*; another the first line of *The Jungle Book*.

First lines can tell you a great deal about the type of story you are going to read.

All my first line of this chapter tells you is that as it *is* a super first line for a book I have used it! I'll tell you what happened at Market Drayton in another chapter. Swanwick was a highlight in Chita's life with me, so that comes first.

This summer of 1983 presented hazards for those of us who travel with our dogs. Cars become unbearably hot and dogs can die in them. Their body temperature is higher than ours (over 101°F) and they need more air than we do; so it is very important to make sure when travelling that the dog is comfortable and not distressed.

I had just changed my car and now have a Vauxhall Astra which has a roof that will open, so that is one advantage. It was necessary to plan the journey, as much as I was able, to keep us both cool. It was a scorching hot day and Swanwick is near Matlock; a journey over moors, and even though we were high, it was windless and airless. I stopped a number of times to open up the car, walk Chita and give her a drink. I carry a large container of water and if it's too hot, soak towels and put them over her to cool her.

I arrived at about four. I did not know anyone but Mike, though I was very soon made welcome by Philippa Boland, who is the widow of John Boland and is now Swanwick Summer School secretary. John is probably best remembered by his book and film *The League of Gentlemen*.

I was told I could put my car where I liked and I found a perfect place, up a path between very high shrubs, so that the sun never shone there at all during any part of the day. It kept the car wonderfully cool. There was so much to do, and such huge grounds, with a shop and bookshop on the site, that I did not move the car until the end of the week. We never went outside the grounds, yet could walk miles in them, and had the use of several fields where I went early to train Chita.

The Hayes Centre is used for conferences of all kinds. It is an enormous house and Nancy Martin, who was probably one of the oldest members there, and also one of the happiest and most lively, in spite of breaking her wrist in a fall on her second day, has written not only the story of Swanwick as a Writers' School, but also of the history of the place, in a book called *Venture of Faith*. Nancy was founder secretary of the Writers' School and much of its success is due to her and those with her who fought to get it going and keep it going.

This is not the story of the Summer School, but I will use Nancy's book briefly to describe the Hayes Centre itself. It is a vast building, with conservatories, a vinery, and enormous public rooms. The entrance hall is so big that I took Chita there to practise her heelwork and stays, and wished I could have premises as large for my own dog club.

There is a wonderful lecture hall that seats over three hundred people very comfortably; and a number of other rooms that are ideal for smaller groups. There is a bar, a dance hall and a swimming pool. Our host for the week, Ronald Whiting, is part of the Hamlyn Publishing Group, and gave us some interesting talks that were immensely helpful to all would-be authors and existing authors. He went swimming one afternoon and came into the Committee Room in his trunks and towel, his soaking wet hair plastered against his head. Chita didn't recognise him in undress, soaking wet. It is the only time she barked at anyone in the Committee Room. She was not even very sure of him when he spoke to her. Possibly he smelled of chlorine, something she had never smelled before as Kenneth, if he swims, swims in the sea and I find no pleasure in our chilly waters.

Swanwick brochures about the conference centre describe it as 'probably the largest of its kind in Europe'. It was used as a barracks in World War I. During World War II it started as accommodation for British troops, but then it became a prisoner-of-war camp for German Air Force officers. Five of these escaped through a tunnel, which has only recently been found.

The first the Summer School Committee knew of the find was in August 1981 when Wally Milne, who runs the place with incredible efficiency and a terrific sense of humour, greeted them as they arrived with the news that it had been discovered. I meant to go and see it, but somehow there was never enough time, as when I wasn't busy with some part of the courses during the week, Chita had to be exercised. I couldn't ignore her needs.

There is also reputed to be a ghost.

I learned all this during my stay.

Mike came to greet me and carried my cases, and then Chita was taken out of the car and I gave her a short walk. She was fascinated by the place; there were two cats; there were squirrels; there were no other dogs and there were more people than she had ever seen gathered together in her life.

I kept her on her lead. She behaves beautifully on-lead, and soon realised that this was an occasion on which she must not let me down. We started by finding a remote and unused path with a dense shrubbery for her, where she was taken throughout the stay, so that she knew this was the only place she was allowed to use for her own needs. I could bury everything under thick piles of humus and leaves and we would not be a nuisance to anyone.

Mike had told me to bring her with me to the Committee Room at teatime, which was four-thirty. Coaches were arriving from the big cities as we went in, and people and luggage were being unloaded. Chita had not seen coaches close to before and was fascinated. They were so big! It was hard to get her past them. People looked rather surprised to see a dog, but someone said 'how lovely; all that's needed to make it feel like home,' as we passed.

It is very daunting to meet so many new people; but I assumed that many would be as nervous as I, which made it easier, and having Chita with me was wonderful as I wasn't alone; I had a familiar companion who fits in with my moods. Also it was soon very plain that people weren't just friendly; they went out of their way to make newcomers feel welcome.

I had asked everyone to ignore Chita. They admired her but nobody fussed her and she soon realised that in the Committee Room she was expected to lie down and remain quiet. She curled by my feet or behind my chair and it was difficult to remember I had a dog with me, she was so good. By the end of the week she was lying on the hearthrug as if she were at home, without her lead, and not once did she get up and roam round the room.

CHAPTER FIFTEEN

Swanwick teas are a dieter's undoing, and they were mine. Homemade bread; country butter; homemade jam; and the most fabulous rock cakes, freshly baked each day. I don't think anyone was able to resist them.

I soon established a pattern for Chita. After tea we went for a walk, usually through the woods. We invariably met the other conference members and our woodland walks were highlights, with talk of books and writers and writing that no writer can get anywhere else. Few of us ever meet. Writing is a solitary business and if we spend too much time talking, we never get any work done.

I did not realise it then but it was a new phase in training for Chita. We never walk with others at home. We either train with others, or alone, or walk alone, or with Janus. At first she was uncertain of her position; next to me, away from other people? Soon she discovered that no matter who I walked with, or who I talked with, she was expected to walk properly, not to pull, and to ignore other distractions, such as the many squirrels and the two rabbits. She watched, fascinated, but did not try to chase.

After our walk it was her feeding time; something that takes about five minutes! Her bowl of food; followed by three small dog biscuits, half a slice of brown bread, and a piece of cheese. Janus started the routine and it must be followed or the dogs feel they have missed something.

Within a day of our arrival Chita knew that when we came in from our walk after tea, we did not go up one flight of stairs and turn right and then walk down the passage to the Committee Room. We went up two flights of stairs to our bedroom. She did not need me to show her the room, as I went up first with the luggage, and then went down to take her up with me. As soon as she reached the corridor she put her nose down and tracked me to the right door, pulling towards it before I had quite reached it.

By the end of the week, if I were sure nobody was about, I let her off her lead at the top of the first staircase and watched her run up the second, into the corridor, straight to the door of our room and sit there of her own accord waiting for me to reach her. Once inside, over to the wardrobe where her food was kept and point her nose at that, and look at me to tell me. Feed me! It's time.

It was just as well Chita's needs as well as my own kept me going up and down all those flights of stairs, as the food was so good that I might well have gained half a stone; and having just lost half a stone, I didn't want that!

She knew that, after her meal, we went for a short walk and then we went to the car. She knew at coffeetime and teatime that we turned right instead of continuing up stairs, and once, when I turned the wrong way, not thinking, I was given a sharp jerk as she pulled on her lead to turn in the correct direction. Where are you going? It's this way. She was quite right; it was.

People soon began to remind me to 'steal' a piece of brown bread at teatime for Chita! The room where we slept was huge. It overlooked the ballroom and gardens. In spite of two beds, an enormous wardrobe and old-fashioned chest of drawers and a washbasin, there was plenty of room for Chita's sleeping mat.

When I travel with the dogs I always carry their

rugs with me. This shows them that we are staying and it is also a familiar part of their lives, a piece of home, and they settle much more quickly in strange places. I also have rugs in the car, as that makes them lie quietly as they do in their own beds and not fuss about while I am driving.

The Hayes Centre is very good accommodation but it is not a luxury hotel. We made our own beds. The food is excellent but it is self-service. It was rather like going back to school, and was great fun, especially as people made inroads on leftovers for midnight feasts! There was always more than enough for this and I suspect it is part of a tradition that Wally Milne knows well and caters for.

Most of us shed responsibility; we were in a sheltered environment and a different world and everyone entered into the spirit of the place.

Mike Legat wrote an article in *The Author* entitled 'The Magic of Swanwick'. It is there and it is impossible to describe to anyone who has not experienced it. Perhaps it is because we all have the same interests; we all write or want to write and talk of ways and means, of methods and ideas, of technique and plotting, of grammar and first lines, of introductions and prefaces, flowed all week without stopping.

We share experiences: the mental blocks when words won't come; the book we start that never works out right; the book we wrote that nobody wanted to buy; the curt little soul-destroying rejection slip on the mat. Mary Wibberley, who has sold more than eighty million copies of her very popular books, spoke of her early rejections, which she shared with the rest of us.

We all talked of rejection; of problems and difficulties as it isn't easy. My bugbear is my computer. The typewriter was bad enough but my little word processor, which is only a glorified typewriter, has dreadful habits and suddenly, just as I am in full flow, it either packs up, or there is a power cut, or it announces BAD COMMAND or SYNTAX ERROR (whatever *that* is!) and throws me completely. There was a computer expert there, but with Chita's needs to cater for I didn't manage to get to any of her talks; and we all felt that those of us with experience, rather than grouping together, should talk to those with less, as we could help them, and that is what we were there for.

So many people have helped me in the past that I want to help others in return for my good fortune.

Chita and I frequently set out to go somewhere and were waylaid by someone who wanted to talk to me, by an interesting sideline, by a group who drew me into their discussion. 'I started but got waylaid' was the week's catchphrase.

Chita slept in the car while we had dinner and then the evening lecture. Her car rug is there and she regards the vehicle as her second home; the most expensive kennel in the country! As we were on private grounds I could leave the windows well open and it was cool up her alleyway.

It meant I had to rush, as I had to change for the evening. This was very flexible. Few of the men did more than put on clean clothes; some wore suits. Some of the women had gorgeous dresses, but I never go to functions where I have to dress up these days; time seems so short and there is so much I want to do. My evening wear is invariably velvet pants and frilly blouse and fancy jacket.

We had before-dinner drinks in the Committee Room and this was followed by our meal. Mealtimes were equally full of conversation on topics of all kinds, but all to do with writing.

The meal was followed by the evening lecture. Lectures were given by publishers, by a libel lawyer, by various authors. The spread of subjects was very wide. After the lecture Chita came out of the car and up to the Committee Room, where we had coffee as there was no time after our meal and before the lecture. Often Chita and I then went down to the bookroom; I spent a fortune on other people's books, most of which I got signed by their writers. With Chita lying beside me, I was part of a number of different groups, never quite knowing who I was going to meet that evening.

One member raced Greyhounds; another trained gundogs; several had dogs and I found myself giving as much advice on dog training as on writing. Our last chore was our nightly walk. The first night I went down the drive to the gate with a dog that started at every shadow. I suddenly realised she had never seen streetlamps except from the car window; she couldn't understand the shadow that grew and shortened as she approached and she didn't like it at all. She spooked all the way and barked as the bushes moved. So we left that walk and went towards the house and back to the shrubbery, using the car's headlights to give us enough light. That she does understand.

'Did she enjoy her walk?' someone asked as we came into the building.

'Streetlamps worried her; she has never seen them before,' I said.

'Where on earth do you live? What kind of place has no streetlamps?'

I found the remark rather sad as the speaker must have led a remarkably restricted life; streetlamps are a rarity to me these days; few of our villages have them and when we stay overnight for Trials we are seldom in a town.

Those who wish to write do need to mix with all kinds of people; nothing can be written if you live in an ivory tower as nothing can ever happen to trigger ideas. I seem to lead an adventurous life compared with many other people. 'Things always happen to you,' a friend said. They only happen because I lead a very full life and sometimes things are bound to go wrong! The mishaps are much more likely to lead to a story than what a small boy I know calls the 'haps'!

Bed, which at the end of what seemed very hectic days was more than welcome, proved to have an unexpected hazard as the dancing went on until one thirty. It was no use trying to sleep. I read, luckily with a renewable source of literature downstairs in the bookshop. I have never done so much bedtime reading in my life. When the dancing ended voices called to one another. 'Goodnight', 'See you tomorrow.'

I had to persuade Chita nobody wanted her to join in and bark her goodnights too, as there were people in the rooms on either side of me and they might have been able to sleep through the music. (I need deep countryside peace before I sleep!)

One of my Swanwick memories is of a small cold nose pushed into my hand every night at 1.30 am as Chita tried to convince me she really ought to bark and tell all those people it was late and they were disturbing her sleep! My last words to her were never 'goodnight Chita', but 'Chita SHHHHHH!'

She learns rapidly and she very soon learned that we got up at six in the morning for her benefit. There was no way I could expect her to lead a prosaic existence all day unless she was well exercised. The morning also began with 'Chita SHHHH', as she gets very excited and squeals when we are going to do something interesting. By the second day she had learned that six in the morning meant something very interesting indeed.

We had to creep down the corridors in order not to wake those still sleeping, and it was hard not to laugh as she seemed, very quickly, to understand we were doing something rather nefarious and seemed to walk on tip-paw beside me, looking up at me for approval. She has learned also that she comes up stairs beside me at my pace, and down stairs behind me, her nose against my knee, so that she can't possibly pull suddenly and send me hurtling headlong. Each flight was long and steep and I had no desire to end up another casualty. Nancy never complained about her arm, but it did make life very inconvenient for her, as she needed assistance when dressing. Another injured writer, this time with perhaps a broken leg, would not add to Swanwick fun!

Walks don't interest Chita. Her reward is always to train with me, to work with me, to be my partner. This is ecstacy and her pride grows with her achievements.

That first morning I looked at acres of ground and laid her a track. It was a fairly easy track, shaped in a square, each side two hundred yards long, with her much-beloved toy (a ball inside a leather glove she chewed up in her puppy days) at the end of it. I took her out of the car expecting instant success.

I had laid the track well away from both the main house and the garden house, as there is no way I can stop the squeals of excitement when she sees her tracking harness. On with the harness and off we go for her to try and find the track.

Tracking is simple when you understand it! When we walk over the ground we leave scent from our bodies, scent from our shoes and we also leave ground scent, made up of the smell of broken and bruised vegetation. The dog is taught to identify the path along which a person has walked and to know the difference between trodden ground and untrodden ground.

A dog sniffing around isn't tracking. It is going from one smell to another. The scent left by another dog; every dog will inspect this as it gives information as to sex, and possibly also breed and age. I don't like my dogs sniffing as they may discover a mess left by a dog sickening for distemper or parvovirus in which case they will develop the disease, even if inoculated sometimes.

Or a lamppost annointed by a dog carrying leptospirosis which is rat-borne and a killer. I have known an inoculated bitch die of this two days after her pups were born. The infection was thought to have come from infected dogfood.

Dogs may roll in a drunk's vomit; they are not discriminating. There is nothing more wonderful than to roll on a dead animal. The stink of a dog that has done this is indescribable so my dogs are trained *not* to rush round sniffing at everything. There is no need; it isn't a crucial part of their existence and it can be dangerous.

The Jack Russell we meet wandering alone on one of our regular walks at home eats anything he comes across; we have found him eating a long-dead rabbit; parts of very dead seagulls; he probably has worms badly, and he may well end up by eating a mouse that has died of warfarin poisoning and dying himself. Both my cats nearly died when they caught mice that had eaten Warfarin.

Two local dogs picked up strychnine bait laid for foxes (which is illegal but is done) and a friend's bitch, in Ireland, died of strychnine poisoning. The doctored carcase of a lamb had been laid on private ground for foxes, but crows had been at it, and one of them had dropped part of its trophy in the road. The little bitch died in agony.

Here there are traps for foxes in some areas; a dog could easily be killed by them and they are meant to kill, not to capture them alive. If dogs wander they may meet any of these; and also if they stray too far from you.

My dog is also my protector; I want her near in case there is danger about. We live in dangerous times; we hear daily of mugging and mayhem and murder; a dog miles away racing off on its own business is useless; mine must be near me, ready to help me do battle.

So Chita is my partner, working with me, as a

police dog works with its handler. She does have her freedom; her favourite game is to race out after her 'mouse', which is a stuffed soft toy made by Roy Hunter who used to help train the Metropolitan Police dogs and now runs the Abelard Academy of Dog Training, in Essex. She and I can play fetch with this for as long as I can stand it; she could go on much longer.

I took her to the track. It ought to have been easy at her stage but she was soon bewildered; it wasn't until the next morning that I found out why!

CHAPTER SIXTEEN

I knew from Chita's behaviour that there was something odd about that field. It might be foxes; or rabbits, though there were no telltale droppings that I could find. She was plainly bewildered so I took her to the end of it, let her find her trophy and played a game with her.

Tracking, at least there, seemed out of the question. It was a good field, on two levels. Some fifty yards in, there was an eighteen-inch drop bounded by a wall. I could throw her mouse down the drop and outwards for some distance, so that she took a flying leap to get to it and another to come back, giving her extra exercise and jumping practice all in one. It was a gorgeous game and she didn't want to stop.

I didn't know what was wrong with the field, as regards tracking, but did know I needed to get up earlier next day and see if I could discover a reason for her failure. Tracking is never easy for the human partner; it is better to try and find out what has happened, so that the dog can be shown, if necessary and if possible, where it has gone wrong.

We went on to practise our Trials heelwork, with Chita at my side, keeping her shoulder by my knee, walking first at a very slow pace, then at a normal walking pace, and finally we jogged all the way to the gate and back. This was a distance of about five hundred yards. Good for both of us! At one point one of the Conference members stood watching me, I thought perhaps finding us rather odd. Later it turned out that he was absolutely fascinated by our training, and thought Chita wonderful; he was pleased to discover he could smile and wish us good morning without disturbing us. He came across to talk to me just before lunch, when Chita was in the car.

She ignored all interruptions; this was her time of day and she was going to have full benefit of it. I had her hurdle with me and also her tunnel. She retrieved her dumbbell over the hurdle and brought it back to me, sitting in front of me, waiting until I took it from her. It was only then I realised we had an audience.

We usually practise alone, so that this was a major benefit, as it taught her to concentrate and work with distractions around her. People weren't standing still; they were walking about, chatting in little groups, passing us, but stopping for a few minutes to watch this rather odd exhibition. Very odd for Swanwick as the Writers' School had seen nothing like Chita's performances before.

Cars were driving past us; the milk float arrived and delivered; the baker's van came. Chita was far too enthralled with her agility to bother; she was full of energy, full of the joy of living, had me all to herself for once, without Janus's needs to be considered too, and was determined to make the most of this unexpected bonus.

Part of the audience was unexpected and was behind me, so I did not see it until too late. Members of the public used the fields to exercise their dogs. A Samoyed bitch ran up to Chita and barked at her, just as she was about to jump. No self-respecting animal will allow such behaviour and before I could take breath Chita was off, chasing the bitch away from her hurdle on to the field. The bitch's owner began to panic and screamed at her dog, so I went over to her and persuaded her to leave them; humans interfering in a fight turn it from a warning to a confrontation. If you leave the animals alone they usually sort matters out without bloodshed; just a lot of noise. The one that makes the most noise wins and the other runs off. That in fact happened. Chita was left victor and came straight to me as the Samoyed ran off. I apologised and leashed her, but if people will let their dogs run free, then they will get trouble.

No dog likes another dog rushing up to it and its owner, and may defend itself, or defend the owner. If it defends the owner it will be a bad fight and if the humans intervene they will make the dogs turn on them; and get very badly bitten. If dogs fight out-of-doors I leave them to it. In club I watch like a hawk to see if one dog dislikes another enough to have a go and, if so, I make very sure both owners are well away from one another, know their dogs don't like one another and don't move suddenly close to one another.

Dog club keeps the trainers very alert. I won't have barking, biting or fighting in my club, ever. We very rarely do have problems as dogs in a group learn not to be aggressive with each other or with people and to accept other dogs. However, if another dog does bark at them or attack them, only an insane dog, however well trained, is going to stand still and get bitten!

We did meet the Samoyed twice more, each time on a lead. Chita was also on her lead and when I saw the other owner and dog approach I made mine lie down. Chita lay still and watched the other owner struggle past, her bitch pulling, out at the end of the lead, up on two legs, roaring defiance at Chita. Chita just looked at me. 'I don't do that, do I?' her eyes said. 'You'd better not,' my eyes told her. We understand one another very well. This procedure also impressed people and I was pleased, because the German Shepherd (Alsatian) has, quite wrongly, a very bad name. Dogs that go wrong usually have owners who have made no attempt to train them and the big breeds *must* be trained.

You can easily pick up a Yorkie or a Westie that is trying to fight, but there is no way you can do anything but use your own control when two animals of larger breeds want to have a go. She was doing good for her breed. A trained German Shepherd is probably better than any other breed, certainly as good as any other breed.

Often those we read of in the press that have bitten weren't even German Shepherds; but crossbred animals, that can be remarkably bad tempered as sometimes the worst of both breeds will come out in a mongrel. I have known far more nasty mongrels than I have pedigree dogs. Some of the crosses that come into club are enough to make you cry, they are so ugly and so difficult to manage. The bitch should have been aborted, not allowed to produce the little monsters that have come from a mismating.

Terriers are fighters, originally bred to kill rats, or fox or badger cubs. The bull breeds are also fighters, originally bred to fight (deliberately bred to fight) bears or bulls. Their flattened muzzles made it less easy for them to get their faces bitten; another animal can hang on to a long muzzle with its teeth.

So that if Terriers and Bull breeds meet and mate there can be real problems, as the fighting instincts are doubled and the resultant dog is so full of mayhem that he never learns to control himself. He attacks anything that moves. I have known a dainty little Jack Russel bitch drag a vixen, still warm, back to the farm. The vixen had bites everywhere and was very dead. The Jackie had one bite on her leg. She was diminutive, but full of fight.

People with Terriers sometimes ask if I know a farmer with a ram that will put the fear of sheep into them by attacking them. The Terrier would very likely enjoy the game enormously and the ram come off worst as Terriers can run rings round them. They fly round the back of the animal, rush in, bite, and are away again fast, out of danger.

When breeders talk of hybrid vigour they aren't talking of the casual mongrel mating. They are talking of a deliberate crossing of two pedigree dogs, specially selected for temperament and health. The result of this is usually wonderful and many breeds started in this way. But it must, like all matings, be done with knowledge and not just to the dog next door.

This was one of the incidental subjects that came up at Swanwick, as people who write are interested in everything; you can write about anything you like from antique clocks to dogs to the habits of a wild community of people in a farout part of the world and provided you know your facts and write interestingly you can make a living from it. So that Chita's training and how we did it was also part of the course, though not on the schedule as such!

Her morning's training was ended by the breakfast bell. She went into the car and I went off about human affairs until eleven o'clock. It was a lovely day, so that we went out on to the lawns and sat drinking coffee. It proved far too hot for both Chita and myself, so we took refuge in the Committee Room where conversations also ranged far and wide, as there were about twenty of us up there. The lecturers, including those who stayed all week and those who only came very briefly to give their lectures, came up there as well as the committee.

The pattern was soon formed. Dogs like routine, and since our days were governed by lecture times and meal times, that suited us very well.

Conference members were very good about not fussing her, though many were dying to stroke her. This is a human attribute that baffles me, possibly because I live so much with dogs that I am well aware that most do not like being fussed by total strangers. They are dignified animals and don't like being treated like puppies. Once the puppy days are over, not many breeds will allow people to fuss them. They stand there, submitting wearily, with no pleasure, and it is unfair. Also many people pat far too hard and may touch a sensitive spot and hurt them.

They don't like their heads being patted. The right way to approach a strange dog is *not* to approach it at all! If you visit a house with a dog that does not rush to greet you just sit quietly and make no overtures whatever. Most dogs will then approach you tentatively and if you reciprocate gently and tickle the dog's chest, telling him, very quietly, he's a good lad, then you have made a friend for life.

Children who rush up to dogs to pat them, or run at them shouting, will get bitten sooner or later. The dog may be trained, but is badly frightened and bites in panic. The plain truth is nobody has ever taught that child how to behave near an animal. I watch at the zoo at times and wonder if parents are insane as tiny hands creep towards the vixen; she will bite if a finger goes through that wire. The monkeys don't like being laughed at; they may hurl things, but they have a weapon they do use in desperation, and can aim a well-directed flow of urine straight into your face if you are stupid with them. Elephants may fill their trunks with water and dowse a noisy human. A baby elephant did it to my small son once when he cried!

So, being used to working with animals, I was very strict with people. One woman said she wanted to pull Chita's tail. I greeted this extraordinary remark with the contempt it deserved, and told her if she did, not only would Chita bite, I would too.

One afternoon I did relax my rule and one of the members fussed Chita and petted her. I did not think our paths likely to cross again. Unfortunately when I went into the Conference Room and took Chita with me, he was sitting on a chair within sight. She wanted to get to him for more petting, and that was the only time she did misbehave. She tried to crawl; I stopped her; she tried to dive and I stopped her; and then she lay and whined, so I had to take her out and put her in the car. I could have gone for a walk but the lecturer might have thought I had walked out because he was boring, which was not the case at all!

The first day passed very smoothly and happily. We were getting used to one another and making friends. The next day was to show me what was odd about our tracking ground and was also to produce one of the silliest incidents of the whole stay, all because I talk to animals.

CHAPTER SEVENTEEN

One of the most daunting parts of Swanwick for me was due to the fact that we live in an isolated area. Our village is small; only 800 people. Our house is down a long lane, without neighbours, and we can go for days without speaking to more than one or two other people. We are both very busy, Kenneth with producing two deepfreezes full of vegetables (this year's speciality being giant pumpkins) and I am busy with writing and the needs of the dogs.

My study window looks across our orchard, which is more a hope than a fact as the winds have taken the blossom every year, except for that on the crabapple tree. Beyond that is a high hedge and then the fields slope upwards to the horizon, which is also hedges, with large trees at intervals. I can see sheep in the fields across the river, sheep the other side of my hedge and this year some pretty little Charollais-cross bullocks belonging to our new neighbour. His house is hidden by the hedge and some distance from ours. Next door means a long walk!

I was trying to describe this on the phone to my Dent publicity department; I was obviously talking to a city-bred girl, as when the book came out I read, to my total amazement, that I have sheep and cattle and a donkey in the garden. I don't! The dogs would eat the dung, and can you imagine our shoes?

I look out on sheep and cattle; not on houses. The donkey belongs to a neighbour; Chita had to be persuaded it had a right there and that she must not bark at it, as she raced up the field yelling 'Go away' and he charged round his field in dismay, finally kicking up his hind heels at her, quite uselessly, as they are separated by a strong pig-wire fence.

I found three hundred and fifty people *en masse* quite overwhelming and was more than glad that I had Chita to walk and could escape to the peace of the woods when my brain grew tired, as it did rather frequently. There was so much talk; there were so many new ideas; so many lectures to digest. Very few others went into the woods. They were lovely, but perhaps others weren't well enough shod to walk there. I prefer comfort to elegance!

It was beautiful weather almost all week; the halcyon summer of 1983. The woods were traversed by paved paths; we wandered idly, looking at shrubs and a tiny lake bordered by a little copse. There were no people and the only sounds were from birds singing.

On the Monday I did get up at six. This was an effort, as the noise of the band and the dancing shuffle and the talk prevented me from sleeping until after two am. Six o'clock seemed to arrive rather fast.

Out and down the corridor, tiptoe and very quiet, Chita SHHH. Out through the doors which were never locked as far as I could see. Out towards our tracking field, and stand quite still and stare. No wonder she couldn't track!

There were joggers, out before they went off to work; and two people with dogs. The field I thought was free from all scent but mine was well and truly fouled before I ever laid her track. Poor Chita. No wonder she had been so bewildered. She was trying to follow my line among a maze of other lines, all recently laid, all crossing and criss-crossing as the joggers circled the field, crossed the field, and some went round the field. I think there were only about four, but they must have left enough track for an army.

So that field was no use at all. I would have to find another. I would need to find out which fields belonged to Swanwick and which to the nextdoor farm. I also needed a field without cattle and there were many of those. On one hilarious occasion those sitting opposite the Conference Room's rear door were startled to see a cow pass, having been separated from her companions and escaped from the field.

Among those in the Committee Room were John Gittings, who works for the publishing firm of Robert Hale, and his wife, Giselle, who had to go home on the Tuesday. Giselle wanted to see the display I had promised to put on with Chita. It meant performing earlier than I had expected, as Mike had already asked if we could do something. It meant very little rehearsal and Chita might not be settled.

So it was necessary to start that day with a full rehearsal and to work out an interesting set of exercises as not all those we do have public appeal. Those aimed at total control are necessarily rather dull for onlookers.

It was again a lovely day and we had a bigger audience than the day before, though few of the Conference members came out before half past seven. This was all to the good as it meant she would have practice with distractions before the actual display. I was pleased with her and hoped she would behave as well at coffee time, which was when we were due to perform.

I must confess I found that morning's lecture a little difficult, as I had my mind filled with the various exercises I needed to give Chita for our own appearance.

After the lecture I fetched the tunnel and hurdle from the car; Swanwick being vast, this was quite a distance away, and I felt rather silly carting a brightly coloured plastic tunnel among so many distinguished and dignified Conference members! I also had the long jump; a stick wrapped up in thick cloth to make a soft baton; the dumbbell; a quoit; and the search articles.

I took titbits which Chita rarely needs now, but dogs are not always predictable and if she failed at any jump, a titbit would give her quick confidence.

I had an unexpected ally who wanted to take a video film of us. Chita has been on video before, and this was something she recognised. She is also apt to play to the gallery and pose for the photographer.

We had an early snag as he wanted to film us coming from the car. In order to make sure she did not disgrace us, I wanted to take her into the shrubbery. I thought he would understand why, but, apparently somewhat baffled, he followed, and Chita would not empty herself with an audience. At last I found a thicket that was quite impenetrable (and rather painful as it was brambly) and got the needed result. Rule one when performing with a dog in any way, at a competition, a Trials or anywhere else, is Empty Your Dog. Use a place where you won't cause offence to others. It is not always honoured at shows and Trials which is a pity as it gives all of us a bad name and those of us who are scrupulous resent being branded as inconsiderate when we try so hard not to be.

Nothing would be more likely to alienate people than to have her produce a pile of muck on the croquet lawn because I hadn't remembered her needs.

She did her utmost to please me. She walked at slow, fast and normal pace; I sent her away from me for twenty yards and stopped her each time in a different position; at the sit, the stand and the down. She hurdled; fautlessly. She jumped the nine-foot long jump; she ran through the tunnel, joined me and walked on.

She fetched her dumbbell over the hurdle.

I wanted to show the search but that is not spectacular for any audience, so I invented a variation. I had in my pocket the top of a golfclub (the metal head), a cartridge case, a cork and a piece of carpet. I made her lie down and stay down at the edge of the lawn and put these down at the far side. She was then sent to find each separately, using her nose to search it out, as she couldn't see them, and bring it in. When she dropped it in my hand I threw it over the hurdle for her to retrieve and bring back again, jumping with it in her mouth. She has been taught to hold small objects with her teeth.

This was a wonderful variation and she adored it. She always has trouble with the flat golfclub head and it annoyed her. She flipped it on edge with her paw, picked it up and there was a round of applause. She stood, looking, and with an air that would have graced any prima donna, she flew over the hurdle, sat and presented me with her trophy.

So we did an encore, this time with even more showmanship on her part.

It was time for the next lecture, so I sat Chita and she barked goodbye and received a tremendous round of applause. She swaggered beside me back to the car, this time with plenty of assistance in carrying the gear.

I was especially pleased as there had been several hazards to our performance. At one stage a young cow was frisking at the far end of our arena; a cat walked down the path, luckily unseen by Chita, and she saw a squirrel as she went for one of the search objects, stood, stared and on my command, ignored it. That was a terrific achievement, much more than anything else she had done, but very few of those present realised just what temptation she had had. She is a chaser.

I rewarded her with a tiny piece of cheese and she settled thankfully to sleep. That was tiring, her body said, as she sighed deeply, nose tucked into her tail, eyes watching me, a position that gives her the oddest old-fashioned expression.

She enjoyed plenty of praise just before lunch, so much so that I was late going down. I was hurrying along the terrace when I saw a baby bird that could not fly as its wings were not yet fully feathered. It was in a panic and among the feet of other people, also hurrying because they too were late.

It dodged me, but came back and I almost trod on it. I dodged it, but it was bewildered and came back again, and yet again.

Finally I lost patience and said: 'Oh *do* get out of my way you *stupid* little creature.'

To my utter horror another Conference member gave me an appalled glance and did get out of my way, fast!

I had no idea who she was and couldn't find her to recognise her again so I made a public apology to an unknown member who I had not intended to insult!

I found a field where Chita could track each afternoon without problems from other people fouling it first and continued her training throughout the week.

The week had its own absurdities. One of the lecturers was Ewart Alexander, who among many achievements has written one of the *King's Royal* series. He gave a memorable talk on writing for television and received a standing ovation.

Ewart writes for Channel Four, and speaks Welsh, neither of which facts I knew. I sat beside him at lunch and had with me a letter I wanted to post, written to a club member whose house has a very Welsh name. Ewart glanced at it and said: 'If you don't mind me saying so, you have spelt that wrong!' I wasn't very surprised as I find Welsh extremely difficult though I do try hard. It amused me to think I had shown the envelope to the only Welsh-speaking member among over three hundred and had my inadequacy recognised.

Ewart's lecture was given the evening before I was to speak. He said he was glad it was over. It is daunting for all of us even, I suspect, the most experienced, and few of us are speakers or work as lecturers. This was also a much larger audience than I had ever had before.

'It's all very well for you,' I said. 'I'm the last; all day tomorrow to work up a panic.'

Ewart had used the blackboard and there was no pointer. He had found a stick in the woods, an ordinary rather bent stick, that he flourished when he spoke. He handed it to me. 'Use that; it's lucky,' he said.

It was also a stick and Chita adores sticks. It was as well we made our own beds, as I finally hid it under my eiderdown wrapped in my pyjamas so that Chita shouldn't find it and chew it up.

It reminded me of another occasion, two years before, when we were very new to Working Trials. She was searching her square. This is twenty-five yards square (and looks about ten times as big). It is outlined by four posts and the dog must look for four hidden small objects. the handler must stay outside. It is necessary to watch which way the wind comes, as if you stand and let the wind blow your scent all over the square (or the judge and steward do) it prevents the dog finding, as the square is flooded with human scent.

Chita raced in and found a stick. A large beautiful thick stick; a throw-for-me-to-fetch stick and she trotted out bearing it proudly. Throw it, her eyes commanded.

I couldn't.

If I threw it she wouldn't search at all. If I gave it to the judge she would go to him; and the same if I gave it to the steward. If I threw it away she would go and bring it back. If I threw it over the hedge she would spend all her search time trying to break through and fetch it. I stuck it down the back of my trousers and sent her out again. She found one object and spent the rest of the search time behind me, trying to pull it out of my waistband, ignoring all commands to go and seek.

I came home and spent the next few weeks littering our practice search area with sticks and telling her not to touch them!

So now I had a stick in my room and I didn't want her to become addicted to them again. She is now trained to play with them when I choose, and to ignore them in the search square. I put dozens of sticks in with the articles and encourage her to leave them alone. But that is recent training.

The last speaker on the last night.

I became more and more nervous. Everyone had said everything already. I didn't know what to talk about at all.

I was walking around with a blank mind and Chita beside me, when I saw a couple smile at me. I went over to speak to them and collapsed thankfully into a chair. Chita had had a very brief walk. I had retired to my room and tried desperately to come up with something original as if I wasn't careful I would just repeat what everyone else had said. I was glad I had been there all week. Imagine coming in on the last night and not knowing you were repeating the others!

Nobody had talked about their early experiences or what made them tick, my new friends said. We began to talk round the subject and slowly the ideas began to come. By teatime they were crystallising; I had three rockcakes to try and quell the butterflies, but instead felt slightly sick!

I changed, after feeding Chita and putting her to sleep in the car, into black velvet trousers, a high-necked frilled blouse with a royal-blue velvet ribbon at the throat and my favourite pleated tangerine blazer.

Somebody admired my outfit which helped. I decided not to have my usual glass of sherry but to stick to bitter lemon. I remember little of the meal. There were grapes for our desert; there was often fruit which was lovely and far less stodgy than a pudding.

I took Ewart's stick, and after Mike had introduced me, I waved it, and said, 'I have Ewart's stick for luck, so I know I'll be all right,' Everyone laughed.

I had been afraid I was going to be the great anticlimax. That helped.

The last night at Swanwick; I fetched Chita and went up stairs and found a hilarious party; the food had been 'purloined'. Chita was in her element and I relaxed my rules and she shared sausages and paté (discreetly), though she refused grapes. It was a lovely ending.

By some time after midnight, Swanwick was over. I wonder if Chita remembers it too?

CHAPTER EIGHTEEN

How *did* I come to be marooned at Market Drayton?

That was another part of an author's odd life. I had been asked by the library to go and talk to children there during National Children's Book Week. It was BC, which is Before Chita. I had Puma and Janus with me.

National Children's Book Week happens once a year. It is, in theory, an excellent idea. It is probably in practice very good for the children, as they see the people who write the books and hear how they come to be written.

It is, however, very exhausting for those of us involved. Not all authors agree to take part as writing time is so precious. I doubt if there is any writer that finds it an easy discipline. We work alone; we work at home. The phone interrupts, family interrupts, even a cup of coffee can be brought in just as a sentence has taken shape; the thought flies off and is not recaptured.

Nobody writes a book in a day or so; it takes months and often years. It's essential to sit down at the same time every day and produce something; one day off means it is tempting not to work the next day; and anyone who has tried to give up smoking or start a diet knows the 'I'll start it tomorrow' syndrome.

It is never possible to devote every hour to writing. There are letters to answer; contracts to think about and sign; the post to be dealt with; proofs to correct, and they are urgent and invariably come just when the next book is going well, and you have to wrench your mind back to one that, as far as you are concerned, is in the past.

We are thinking, all the time, into the future. This book, as I write, is due at the publishers in December 1983 for publication in the summer of 1984. By then I will be engaged on the 1985 book. 'Now' for those of us producing books and plays is always a few months ahead!

Our post here is an extra irritation as it is country mail and comes any time between nine and midday; and may have something urgent needing immediate attention. So I must stop and open it.

There are all kinds of snags to visiting schools and libraries that neither the teachers nor the librarians seem to understand. It is easy enough on my home ground to find a place and arrive on time; but when travelling more than thirty miles and ending up in a town with one-way systems and parking restrictions, life becomes impossible to manage. The place I want is invariably miles from the place where I can park my car; or the car park is at the back of a complex one-way system and I only find the turn on the second time round after stopping to ask the way.

Sometimes one is sent a map; this is ideal. Others send a sketch, omitting the little roads and only marking the major roads; but when driving you need to know it is the fourth turning on the right, not the second on the map, with two roads left out! Especially if in heavy traffic.

Often you are inadequately briefed. Oh yes, there is room to exercise your dogs; and I find an immaculate field or a town and there is not room for *my* dogs to empty themselves as I won't allow messes where people walk. It may happen by total accident, but it is not going to happen because I let them go where they please.

This can give major problems as school staff tend

to be mesmerised by time; lesson time. I arrive, having not had time to exercise my dogs because I was anxious not to be late; nowhere to exercise them. I am taken straight into the hall without time to breathe or exercise me! I start straight away, after a hundred-mile journey which no one has considered because they are all local. I have had to get up at five am in order to exercise the dogs first and pack the car, as I do all the things non-authors do, like shopping and cooking and washing and exercising dogs, and also run the dog club and life is often more busy than most people's, as they don't write books as well. If my car isn't as well kept as others it isn't because I am lazy, but because there are simply not enough hours in any day.

Taking dogs to schools has other hazards as some children are so impossible with animals; and very likely to be bitten by even the most placid dog as they race at it screaming, or behave like monkeys, apparently equally uncivilised. At one school I walked in with Puma and Janus, both leashed, both behaving perfectly, and a parent stood up and said: 'How dare you bring a dangerous animal like an Alsatian in among children?' At that point a child raced at us, yelling 'dog, dog, dog,' or something like it and Puma, horrified at such appalling behaviour, promptly got under the table and lay there, looking thoroughly alarmed.

I pointed out that it was not my dogs that lacked manners.

Another school posed problems by only allowing us half an hour for lunch; we had to drive five miles, and the road was up; find somewhere to empty the dogs without causing offence – and eat! The restaurant had been briefed and produced a lovely salad which we swallowed in indecent haste, and rushed off. We were late back at the school because the red lights had caused problems as they were kept red while a lorry unloaded gravel between the lights, and we arrived, feeling slightly sick, as we had, quite literally, eaten in about eight minutes.

We were met by an irate headmaster who hoped, acidly, we had enjoyed our three-course leisurely lunch. He, of course, had eaten on the premises, with no time spent in travelling to a restaurant or seeing to the needs of three dogs, as that was PC, which is Post Chita. He then stalked off. I looked thoughtfully at Chita but decided not to make her growl at him for me!

Another school that invited me omitted to tell me they wanted me to give lessons all day to two classes at a time. I am not a teacher; and I had prepared one talk to give to an audience in the school hall. I was startled to be led into a classroom, left on my own, and have children fed in to me at forty-minute intervals. I was there until seven that night, as they were determined to make the most of my visit and parents were invited to meet me. I might add that on these occasions publishers only pay for petrol and a stay overnight if necessary. Not all publishers do this; sometimes one is expected to do signings for publicity, which can be minimal as the press forget to come and nobody else does either! There was, then, no fee. Again I had a hundred-mile journey back; the day had been advertised correctly to everyone except me!

It puts you off children's events.

Three years ago I went on strike. I now insist on a fee and my expenses.

There are, however, compensations. There was the absolutely wonderful school where I was met and taken to the Headmaster's study and given coffee and sherry; and left to relax for half an hour in an easy chair with the morning paper. The hall was packed with silent children who behaved like angels and were a delight to speak to; and afterwards I was taken to lunch in the domestic science block.

The school had its own flat which the girls learned to care for. Everything was polished till it shone; the table laid with silver and glass, with flowers, and the most beautiful embroidered lace cloth. The girls waited, serving wine as it should be served; and we were regaled with a prawn cocktail; with lamb and roast potatoes and peas and mint sauce; and the most delicious cheesecake. There were mints served with the coffee. It was a meal that would have done credit to a top-quality restaurant, and the girls had cooked it all themselves.

When I left there was a small committee of children in the entrance hall, waiting to thank me and present a large bouquet.

It was an occasion I remember with the greatest of pleasure.

Some of the adult occasions are very little better; you aren't met; aren't given time to unwind from the journey and on some occasions aren't even thanked. At one talk I gave I received a complaint afterwards that I had gone on too long and made someone miss a bus; why she just didn't get up and walk out I shall never know; she wasn't handcuffed to her chair and any speaker understands. It is difficult to time oneself if there is no clock; you can't keep looking at your watch! A sensible chairman will look at his or hers discreetly and catch your eye, or tap the watch to clue you.

The funniest occasion of this sort was at a Mothers' Union meeting. I was to talk about writing and the vicar's wife was to introduce me. She stood up and announced:

'We are very pleased to have the author Joyce Stranger with us today. She is going to talk about her books. I haven't read any as I only read good books.' She then realised what she was inferring and proceeded to make matters far worse, until I was almost speechless with an attempt not to roar with laughter.

I was able to indulge this when I stood up and said:

'I just don't know how to follow such an introduction.' The audience collapsed, and I was able to regain my own balance and go on without feeling impelled to giggle every few minutes. I don't think the poor lady ever knew what she had actually said. The ending was equally disastrous as somebody asked me if I ever tore up what I wrote.

Nobody writes at peak level all the time so I told them about *Chia the Wildcat*; I wrote about nine hundred pages in all as it was a remarkably difficult book to write, mainly due to the fact that my father was dying when I wrote it.

'How many pages are there in the book?'

'About one hundred and eighty.'

'You must be *mad*,' my interrogator said with total conviction.

There isn't an answer to that! It all depends on how you define madness, I suppose. If it is a desire to write something as well as possible, then I am definitely not normal!

One of the problems I find with the very young just starting out on their careers is that they have not yet learned how to be professional. Some people never learn it. It does, however, save you from making major mistakes.

I was invited to talk to children at eight different venues that year. We had just moved; the house was in a shambles as it was gutted inside and being replastered, as well as having new woodwork; there was little I could do, and escape seemed a wonderful idea.

I doubt if it was; as at one point that week I was driving in an early fall of snow in the Lake District along a byroad the RAC had told me was passable when my radio sent out a warning message. Two men had killed a warder with an axe, escaped from prison and stolen a car, and travellers on my road were warned not to stop for any reason whatever if flagged by hitchhikers or other vehicles. It was getting dark. I arrived unnerved.

Fortunately on that occasion to a royal welcome, as Market Drayton had left me feeling decidedly ruffled, vowing never, ever, to take on any kind of public engagement again.

I don't really write any book especially for children. I consider children are adults that have not yet lived as long as the rest of us; they have the ability to understand an adult story and often the longing to be part of a world that they will grow up to inherit. We can't protect them from daily life; we can help them to understand other viewpoints.

I discovered long ago that children read my adult books and often read them with more under-standing than some adults. Children are realists. I sometimes receive letters that baffle me. 'I saw your book on the bookstand and bought it for my little son. He likes animals.'

Animals are not for children! My books are about adults; not children; about adult lives and preoccupations. The farmer leads a life far tougher than that of most city dwellers; he is concerned with birth and death, with sudden disaster, with finance, as animals mean profit or loss. The sheep killed by pet dogs mean a loss of income for the man who was attacked; not a small income loss; it could be major if he operates on a tiny margin on a hill farm.

The books sold for children are aimed at adults, but are shorter than the adult books; the age group I am willing to talk to ranges from 12 upwards; sometimes I do talk to younger children, but very rarely as I don't write for them.

Perhaps it is as well some parents think my animal stories are nice little books for their children as some children may never get the chance to read a 'real' book otherwise, but be kept at a level far below their understanding. Children need stretching, not babying. So do dogs! All our dogs could reach a level very little below that attained by the Guide Dogs for the Blind, but how many do in the hands of a pet owner? Poor children. Poor dogs. Their brains are starved.

I do not deal in sex or violence of a sadistic kind in my stories. There is violence; life itself produces its own kind of violence; it comes from fire and flood and human mayhem of the sort a child will understand. Few parents realise the bullying that can go on amongst their little innocents. I remember my own school days; they were far from the happiest time of my life because I did not know how to deal with sadistic girls or sarcastic teachers. Children inhabit a very real world; they need to grow up and learn how to cope with it. There are children of the devil amongst us as well as children of God.

I keep straying from Market Drayton. It was a memorably difficult occasion, remaining vividly in my memory even though it was over seven years ago now, so perhaps I have a psychological reason for wandering from the point!

My talks are written in advance, rehearsed and taped, and then I try to rewrite if it lags or seems dull. It may take a fortnight or more to prepare, and learn, as I don't usually speak from notes. I was ready to talk to children from twelve upwards at Market Drayton.

I was asked to come at twelve o'clock.

It was early closing. Nobody appeared to be at the library, though I finally found a side door and was informed the time had been changed to three pm. I need not have got up at five am if I had known! Could I find something to do? In a town I didn't know, on a dull cold day, for three hours, with all the shops closing? I asked to at least sit in the warm library.

We had lunch in a pub; nobody knew what to talk to me about and the lunch was foul; lager and lime and a very stodgy tepid pie that I hoped wouldn't give me food poisoning. We went back to the library. What on earth would they do with me until three? I could see the wheels ticking. I was invited to sit in on a ladies discussion group on *Wuthering Heights*. It isn't one of my favourite books and it was soon plain that nobody understood how a writer worked at all. Whatever Emily Brontë had had in her mind when she wrote I am sure it wasn't the very odd motives imputed to her.

At one point someone brought me into the discussion. (I had asked not to be introduced.) She looked at me and said 'Why didn't Cathy marry Heathcliffe at the start of the book?' 'Because there wouldn't have been a book!'

I received some startled looks. Finally the library staff came for me to do my bit and introduced me. Was that why I had said what I did? Yes, I said, and thanked them for what had been a very interesting session. It showed me how far out readers can be at times, and what can be read into quite a straightforward story. I rarely have the deep motives that reviewers impart to me and I certainly don't, as one reviewer wrote, have a kink about old men. I love listening to their memories that go back so far, to days before I was born. My grandchildren have the same tendencies. Tell us about when you were a little girl, Gran. It is just telling a story and all of us like that.

World War II isn't history to me; I was there; and the television serials have got most of it wrong, in some way I can't define. It just wasn't like that; it was intensely irritating, it was infuriating, it prevented all of us from carrying on with our own lives, and it was deadly boring.

You listened to a doodle bug go over and when it exploded knew you were safe but somebody else was dead, and there just isn't any way to describe that kind of feeling.

I am still running away from Market Drayton!

I fetched the two dogs from the car and went to meet my audience, expecting to find a group of older children seated quietly in a lecture theatre. What I found was what seemed to be about forty unsupervised five-year-olds running around like lunatics, and was told this was my audience. I very nearly left.

Very plainly, nobody had done any homework. I was a children's author and these were children. Babies need people who write about babies; people used to handling babies, and I am not. Also Puma was appalled by them; they frightened her, and she looked so unhappy she had to go out to the car. I stood there, after I had put her in, wondering whether just to get in and drive away but it wouldn't have endeared me to my publishers, who certainly weren't to blame for the mix-up. My carefully prepared talk was useless; two weeks of work was wasted; I could have been better employed, and I had to nerve myself to take Janus and go back and face a children's party.

I don't like adult parties. A children's party is my idea of total hell. Imagine asking anyone to come without warning to take charge of such an event.

What on earth was I to do with them? I couldn't tell them a story as I don't tell stories aloud off the cuff and I wasn't going to try and remember the traditional stories. You have to rehearse that kind of thing. And I am not an actress.

In the end I sat them all on the floor and 'trained' Janus to nursery rhymes which they all sang for me. He found it decidedly odd; every move he made told me so; this wasn't what he understood. That made two of us! Finally I put him in a down position and let the children walk in single file round him. I don't think it was a successful occasion at all; the children would remember Janus and perhaps the afternoon; it did nothing for anyone and convinced me that unless those arranging events in Children's Book Week did their homework properly and took some trouble, the whole thing was a waste of time.

I think I was felt to be unreasonable; but authors are not specialists in childminding, any more than most other people. The only amusing part of the afternoon was a little girl who said to her mother: 'Look, mummy. Those two dogs are the dogs on the front of that book.'

'Don't be silly,' her mother said. 'Those dogs are famous. What would they be doing in Market Drayton.'

I wondered that too. It hadn't occurred to me either, that any of us was famous! It was a remarkably funny thought. That is how I came to be marooned there. It is also why I now vet all engagements very thoroughly indeed!

The week was fraught with difficulty as my engagements covered over seven hundred miles of driving; I told people where I was starting from and they never allowed me enough time for my journey. To add to my memories of Market Drayton the hotel I stayed in, which was not in the town, would not let me out until 8 am! The door was locked and breakfast was at eight. I had asked for it early, and the landlord said NO. Loudly and firmly. I arrived downstairs at seven hoping to make him change his mind and found he had changed his mind. There was bacon and egg and coffee and toast.

Delighted, I sat down to eat.

He came in and stared at me. 'That's *my* breakfast.'

He didn't think it at all funny. I did! By then it was too late to do anything but let me finish it, as I had made a good start and the egg and bacon plate was empty.

It made him even more determined not to open the main door which was locked with a giant key, kept by the landlord, until eight o'clock. I only hoped the dogs would understand as neither could get outside. They were in my room. I half expected puddles on the floor, but they did manage; just. They both bolted to the nearest patch of grass with deep sighs of relief and I chalked up cruelty as well as bad manners – and that is a hotel I never will visit again.

They aren't all like that. Only last weekend I stayed at a little hotel in Cleobury Mortimer where the landlord fell in love with Chita; she was allowed everywhere I went and nobody could have gone to more trouble for us. A place I will recommend and return to with pleasure. Everyone was delightfully friendly.

I had to travel to the Lake District that day; I travelled fast and even then was late; I, of course, was blamed. Nobody could be detained against their wish in a hotel! They can be; apart from anything else it took a remarkable time to make out my bill. People can be very clever at making themselves as awkward and uncooperative as possible.

At the start of that week I had been asked to go and talk at another library; when I arrived I discovered I had once more only been half-briefed, and was to go on to another nearby in the afternoon. Both were a complete waste of my time. Both were in shopping precincts; the audience, on each occasion, was of tiny children left by their mothers while they went to the shops, delighted to find an attraction there. In the morning there was a pantomime before I was to speak; a lot of noise and shouting, giants and goblins; and the dogs had to be hurriedly taken out to the car.

I forget what I spoke about; it didn't really matter as the children had had enough and were racing about or crying for their mothers, and nobody seemed to be bothered as to what I was there for or whether I spoke or not. They liked Janus; Puma refused to come in.

I was taken out to lunch and on again to another

precinct. I had to ring home to say I was going to be late. I hadn't expected a second session. It was advertised but the author is often the last to be briefed; they remember everybody else! Again there was a pantomime which I was expected to sit through and again I wasn't told till too late. I had to take Puma out to the car and discovered I was in the middle of what appeared to be a major police exercise.

It turned out that the National Front had organised a parade. There were about six of them and about sixty policemen! I had a somewhat hilarious walk to the car with a police escort.

Back in the hall, I once more, with an audience of tinies, 'trained' Janus to nursery rhymes.

Librarians often find me pernickety as I now ask a lot of questions, but I simply don't have time to waste on occasions like that. I have far too much to do, and books to write, and am better employed in that than in minding children dumped while mother goes shopping!

Sometimes I am sad when I say no to an engagement. I was asked to present prizes at a school where my books are popular. It is nearly two hundred miles away from me; it would involve a long drive and two nights stay at the town I am visiting; the purchase of new clothes as I don't have anything right for that sort of occasion, and a day spent in having my hair done before I went. In all a week would be gone from my life for the sake of one afternoon. It is very difficult for people to realise that those of us who write don't lead lives of leisure.

Writing for a living is one of the most demanding tasks there is.

Nor do we make the kind of money that one sees reported as given for books by people who aren't writers at all. All kinds of people in the public eye receive vast sums of money for their life stories. It often seems unfair. If we were to become famed for some absurdity like pushing a piano naked up

Snowdon we would make far more than we do by writing the kind of story our readers like to read! Or commit a crime and cash in by selling the story to the Sunday Dreadfuls.

As a policeman friend of mine often says: 'There ain't no justice!'

On occasions such as that at Market Drayton I often feel there ain't no sanity neither!

One thing, you won't catch me being marooned there again!

CHAPTER NINETEEN

Very few people now have known Chita since her puppy days. One of the few is John Grantham, who judged her four years ago and found the occasion so memorable it now forms one of his topics of conversation. I meet him and his wife when I go to Trials, as all judges are also competitors, and look at his four dogs, steady, sensible and all working dogs with lovely temperaments, able to qualify to a high degree in Trials. Both he and his wife Irene work their dogs and have qualfied them right through the stakes in the past. They are now working new young dogs. He paid me one of the greatest compliments I have had in a long time, when he told me one of his bitches is due to be mated on her next season.

I can't manage another pup yet; I don't have time. It would not get the training it deserved or the amount of time I feel necessary for my dogs; Janus. is old and has his own needs; he can't be left all the time as the dog by the fireside; he adores walking, even if he is now very slow, and being with me. Chita needs far more time for training and exercise than the majority of dogs and until I have her to a much higher standard, and do not have so many writing commitments, she will remain my only dog when Janus goes.

I said, rather wistfully, to John: 'I would love another pup. One day, would you let me have one of yours?' He answered: 'Joyce, I'd love you to have one of my pups.'

John's last letter to me pleased me very much. He writes:

> When I was first introduced to Chita it was at the Yorkshire Working Trial, when I was judging control in UD. The dog was uncontrollable after you left her with my wife as steward in the ten-minute downstay, handlers out of sight.

(I did a second attempt at the stay with Chita on the lead and Irene trying to hold her, as John felt I needed some help with this exercise and hoped that a repeat with another group on-lead might get progress.)

John goes on:

> She just would not keep still and what with the dog pulling to get back to the handler, nearly choking herself, my wife just could not hold her, so I took her, hoping to be able to keep her in the down position.
>
> Chita was the same with me, really going berserk to get back to her owner. It was just unbelievable. But now after three years Chita is much more controlled and anyone who knew Chita will know what a lot of Hard Work her owner has done with her. The out-of-sight ten-minute downstay is still a problem as she cannot bear her owner to go out of her sight, but I hope that the stay will click one day soon, and then Chita will definitely be qualifying in Working Trials.
>
> I do know that Chita will always stay with her owner in sight and has done a sponsored down.

I am hoping that by going to different groups, training with different dogs, and also with other people than those I know well here, we will both be able to accept new environments more easily, as a dog will always behave well in a place it knows among people it knows, but does have to be *taught* to accept new situations. Dogs are very much creatures of routine.

Many people do not realise that you can teach the ten-minute stay to a foolproof state in club, at home, and in say Llandudno. Take the dog to Holyhead and it has never done a stay there for ten minutes, so you must go back to doing one-minute on-lead and build it up, as it does not associate the new place with the exercise. Dogs that go around a lot and are taught their show work in a great many different areas are not as easily put out by new places as those who are unable to travel.

I live in isolation and train alone; a place in which there are fifty or sixty dogs she has never met before, with strange sights such as a motorway bridge near the competition venue, or an overhead footbridge, or a level crossing with gates going up and down can all put any dog off its stroke or worry it.

When tracking it's vital to go back to baby tracks occasionally to help build the dog's confidence; when teaching the stay, go back to short ones, stays on lead, as well as to build very gradually to out of sight, always stopping if the dog is distressed as an upset dog will *not* perform properly.

Police dogs are taken back to basics frequently; they return for retraining stays. A dog that has not tracked for six months will have forgotten how; try not driving for six months and then starting again, or playing tennis again after a two-year layoff; you won't be anywhere near crack performance. Yet dogs are expected to learn and remember for years when humans can't!

Some other Chita letters came from Swanwick members who bought *Three's A Pack* while I was there, and heard my lecture.

Lucia White wrote: 'I'm finding your struggle with

Chita fascinating and who would believe that beautiful creature could ever have been such a little monster?'

She continues:

I must say I was amazed when I first saw Chita crossing the lawn as dogs have been strictly forbidden at Swanwick...but of course I did not know Chita then, Chita is in a bracket all on her own. My initial surprise was quickly followed by admiration. Here was an Alsatian bitch in prime condition, coat thick, eyes bright, ears cocked and all the time her alert gaze taking in your every movement. Even to the least doggy among us it must have been apparent how much she was enjoying her life.

Because of this very striking first impression, I was amazed, on reading *Three's A Pack*, to learn about her early behaviour. I could not believe that the animal you described so vividly, a sheer "Hell Hound" if ever there was one, aggressive and vicious (which she was with other dogs J.S.) could have become the elegant, impeccably mannered Chita that I had the pleasure of meeting. Even now as I remember her going joyfully through her paces on that sunlit lawn, watched by close on three hundred people, and oblivious to them all except her mistress, it seems so impossible. Could she really have been so wicked? So ready to bite and snap and howl? You certainly worked a miracle with her. I wish you had been around to advise me on my naughty Harvey.

You have a great gift of perseverance and patience and above all else love, otherwise the story of Chita would not have had a happy ending. I'm sure if Chita had fallen into anyone else's hands the end would have been tragedy and this beautiful creature would have been given a one-way ticket to the vet's.

Lucia is not the only person who has voiced this opinion and sadly I know a number of dogs of Chita's breed, that have had to die, that I am sure would not have died if they had been mine as I would have *trained* them; not left them to grow up untutored, never knowing right from wrong and unable to understand the unpredictable vagaries of their all-too-human owners, who did not ever understand their dogs.

Elizabeth Elgin (a fellow contributor to *My Weekly*) did not see much of Chita as she was a steward at Swanwick but she said in a letter to me: 'I must say that little hell hound in *Three's A Pack* bore no resemblance to the lovely shadow at your heels. I wish I had read the book before Chita came to Swanwick. I would have found it hard to accept.'

It was lovely to hear from people who had enjoyed both the books and my talk; I was sure it had been boring in the extreme as I am so different in background to most writers; very few of us live in the country and write on country matters. Even when I lived in a suburb I escaped every afternoon to farm or kennel or stable, or the woods and nature reserves nearby.

Another member who wrote to me was Dolly Sewell who starts her letter:

'It was a most unusual sight. My twenty-fourth consecutive year at the Writers' Summer School but the first time I had ever seen anyone there with a dog.'

She goes on to say she has been a long-time fan; no writer can ever resist that! She maybe sums up what I am trying to do in my books so I will quote her though that is not about Chita. She is obviously the kind of reader I am trying to reach and do reach, and that is something all writers need!

She says:

Joyce's books are always about animals but they involve human characters too. I know no other writer who writes so authoritatively and so understandingly about animals. She has an uncanny knack of being able to get inside their skins. She cannot only feel fear, but smell it; feel hungry and know the instinct to kill; to follow scents and trails; to need affection maybe. In her novels she seems able to think with the mind of the animal. A rare talent, an admirable one. Yet never sentimental. Depth of feeling but never sentimentality.

She writes with the same feeling about people. About the farmer, aware that foot and mouth disease is only a whisper on the wind away, and he seeks solace in the bottle; a policeman whose police dog has died; a girl who has given her heart to a horse; a disillusioned newspaper man writing of death and human tragedy to read over the toast and marmalade.

To read one of her books is to become involved. Always.

Had she brought almost any animal it would have been in character. For Joyce Stranger is synonymous with animals. Such a small woman yet packed with dynamite. (Wow! I hope not! I don't often explode! Only with people who abuse me or my dog; never with dogs.)

Chita is a fine looking six-year-old. Even when resting and apparently at peace, her dark ears are cocked, ever-ready. I felt that it only needed one word to have her springing up, eager to chase a ball or a bone or engage in a spot of training.

But probably the biggest test of the animal's training was being with around 370 people for six whole days. Throughout the entire time Chita behaved perfectly. She *watched* squirrels scampering across the grass and up tree trunks. (They were tame J.S.) She *watched* birds walk across the lawn. She *watched* people walking about, talking, laughing, drinking numerous cups of coffee. My guess is she'd have loved to have joined in everything: barking at the birds, tracking the squirrels, sharing biscuits with the coffee-drinkers. But she had been trained correctly.

It was not till later when I read *Three's A Pack* that I learned the full story of the training (though taming might be a more appropriate word) of Chita. Some odd incidence of genes had implanted a demon in that doggy breast. As a pup it tried to master Joyce. For months and months on end its fiendish ways nearly drove its owner to distraction. But this small woman was not going to give in. This boss dog was not going to boss her.

The result was there, at Swanwick, for all to see. Not only was Joyce the boss, but she and Chita obviously have a terrific personal relationship. There was a bond between pet and pet owner.

Dolly went on to talk about my lecture. As it had worried me so much I will quote part of that too as she said:

Joyce held her audience from the first word she spoke. She told us many of her amazing experiences with animals.

Throughout her talk there was absolute silence. When she finished the applause was terrific.

Chita was in the car on that occasion; I finished up punch drunk and totally exhausted; but one thing I did know. A writer is very rarely lucky enough to have such an audience as everyone there without exception has in a small or a big way shared the same experiences; we all work with words and play with words; we all try to write tales that will appeal to people who want to read more; we all have our own passions and no good writer can ever write without an urgent need to impart some part of his own philosophy to others; and we all know what it is like to be rejected, even top writers!

Maybe we have a passionate desire to put the world to rights; or a need to tell others of a part of life few know about, as few people now understand animals, or live with them as they should live; those who come to me for teaching often say after reading my book *How to Get a Sensible Dog*: 'I've had a number of dogs, but I had never understood the dog before; I thought he knew things he can't know.'

I owe Chita's continued existence to a number of people who have helped me, but as with my books which can't be sold unless I write them, I couldn't have done it without my own major contribution. Helene's father said Toby owes his life to me; he does, but my part was *very* small because Helene worked and Helene fought his nature and Helene turned him into a biddable dog; she did all I taught her. Had she not done so, Toby would be dead. Had I not done so, Chita would never had lived through her first two years. The working breeds *must* be worked, and a fighting Terrier is as much a working breed as a guarding Dobermann, or gundog bred to go out with the man who shoots or the Collie that is bred for working the sheep on the hill. A dog deprived of its job is as unhappy as an unemployed human and more likely to go bad.

I am grateful to all those who helped me but I am stressing my own major part in Chita's rehabilitation because I teach others myself these days. I can teach till the moon turns blue and elephants fly and fish live on land, but nothing I say will have the least effect until I can carry my pupils with me, can inspire *them* with the desire to go on and train; to give their dogs good lives. I have to make them realise that in the end it is up to *them*; theirs is the credit not mine. I showed the path. They had to follow it.

It has never been easy and it isn't easy now. I train in rain and I train when I am tired and I train when it is hard to find a moment away from my home responsibilities and my work. I go back to earlier stages again and again to try and make Chita understand something I must have been teaching her badly. Her mistakes are not her own; they are of my making. I have failed to communicate.

Chita may never win any prizes; may never win any titles; but she will remain in many people's memory, and I know that through her others have kept and begun to train dogs they thought were villains and learned the unique pleasure that only comes to those of us who turn a dog into a teammate.

Chita, COME. Let's go and look in that post box and see what's there. A letter from Ross? A letter from America talking about books and dog training? A letter from someone in England wanting help with yet another dog?

What in fact was there was a letter from Bev Telfer, all the way from New Zealand, and, with her letter, I end this book:

Dear Joyce
What an unbelievable pleasure to meet you and Chita and Janus. Too late for Puma.

After years of knowing you through your books it was very easy to spend half a day talking dogs. My older dog is related to Chita but he was never as wild with the obsessive desire to work nonstop. He is a very geared-up dog when he is working and it has taken me six of his seven years to begin to steady him down in the Obedience ring and at Working Trials.

He tries so hard to please that he is like an over-wound spring – one false move on my part and he is there doing the next move before you are ready.

It is no consolation to always be complimented by the judges on your enthusiastic worker when that very attitude has cost you a barrow-load of points.

Chita was so like Shad in her way of coming as soon as you move off – always watching. Watching her, I realised that she had accepted you as boss and pack leader. She would have been dead by now if she hadn't!

I have taught at our dog training club for a number of years but not come across a dog like Chita, thank goodness. Even at six-years-old that energy remains. Only old age will slow behaviour, I think, although Chita now seems to be well under your control.

Thank you again for a wonderful day. Living on the other side of the world means I will not see Chita or Janus again. If you are still mad enough to be working a dog in ten years time, I hope to call again when my husband and I visit Britain together this time.

Regards
Bev Telfer

THE MONASTERY CAT AND OTHER ANIMALS
by Joyce Stranger

Here, from Joyce Stranger, Britain's best-loved writer of animal stories, are all the animals that she understands and describes so well ... pedigree cats and barnyard strays, working dogs and family pets, wild horses and untamed animals from the sea and the jungle ...

Joyce Stranger can write about animals as no other writer – and make you love them ...

0 552 12044 8   £1.50

CHIA THE WILDCAT
by Joyce Stranger

Chia!

– the sound of the wildcat – as explosive as a gun-shot, as sharp as a slash of claws ...

No tame and gentle fireside tabby, Chia is a prowling savage beast, who comes out of the night to kill. Often the only traces of her presence are stray feathers, blood-spattered bones and her terrifying wails in the night.

The wildcat has no friends, but many enemies, the most feared of which is man. So Chia makes her home far from human haunts, where the looming shadow and the lethal gun of the hunter will not menace her kittens.

But even there the eagle and the fox give her no rest ... and the wild cry rings out over the rolling glens –

Chia!

0 552 09891 4   £1.25

JOYCE STRANGER NOVELS AVAILABLE IN CORGI PAPERBACKS

THE PRICES SHOWN BELOW WERE CORRECT AT THE TIME OF GOING TO PRESS. HOWEVER TRANSWORLD PUBLISHERS RESERVE THE RIGHT TO SHOW NEW RETAIL PRICES ON COVERS WHICH MAY DIFFER FROM THOSE PREVIOUSLY ADVERTISED IN THE TEXT OR ELSEWHERE.

☐ 12481 8	**JOSSE**		£1.50
☐ 07600 7	**THE RUNNING FOXES**		£1.25
☐ 10054 4	**NEVER COUNT APPLES**		£1.25
☐ 10397 7	**NEVER TELL A SECRET**		£1.25
☐ 10927 4	**TWO'S COMPANY**		£1.50
☐ 11210 0	**A WALK IN THE DARK**		£1.50
☐ 11536 3	**THE JANUARY QUEEN**		£1.50
☐ 09891 4	**CHIA THE WILDCAT**		£1.25
☐ 10127 3	**ONE FOR SORROW**		£1.25
☐ 11014 0	**KHAZAN**		£1.50
☐ 09399 8	**A DOG CALLED GELERT**		£1.50
☐ 09462 5	**LAKELAND VET**		£1.25
☐ 09725 X	**WALK A LONELY ROAD**		£1.25
☐ 12044 8	**THE MONASTERY CAT AND OTHER ANIMALS**		£1.50

All these books are available at your book shop or newsagent, or can be ordered direct from the publisher. Just tick the titles you want and fill in the form below.

TRANSWORLD READERS' SERVICE, 61–63 Uxbridge Road, Ealing, London, W5 5SA.

Please send cheque or postal order, not cash. All cheques and postal orders must be in £ sterling and made payable to Transworld Publishers Ltd.

Please allow cost of book(s) plus the following for postage and packing:

U.K./Republic of Ireland Customers:
Orders in excess of £5; no charge
Orders under £5; add 50p

Overseas Customers:
All orders; add £1.50

NAME (Block Letters) ....

ADDRESS ....

....